"It's difficult at any age to be willing to explore the use of alcohol and drugs possibilities of living life in recovery are limitless. I encourage you to choose that option and to use this workbook on the journey toward a better life. *Your Recovery, Your Life for Teens* by Claudia Black is absolutely the resource to take with you on this journey."

> **—Mel Pohl, MD, DFASAM**,
> senior medical consultant for the Pain Recovery Program at The Pointe
> Malibu Recovery Center, and author of *The Pain Antidote*

"This gentle workbook by Claudia Black adds to her impressive oeuvre—training texts, life-story compendia, readers, and therapist trainings, all committed to helping the human spirit overcome illness and trauma. This wonderful addition to her work is for young adults, those in that uncertain place between teenager and adulthood, guiding them with a sure hand from darkness to self-compassion and enlightenment, providing deep insight and healing along the way."

> **—Paul H. Earley, MD, DFASAM**,
> past president of the American Society of Addiction Medicine

"I am deeply impressed by Claudia Black's *Your Recovery, Your Life for Teens*. This comprehensive workbook offers an engaging journey for teens struggling with drugs and alcohol. Black provides compassionate, practical tools for self-awareness, coping skills, family involvement, and self-care. Emphasizing gratitude and a supportive environment, this resource is a valuable gift for teens seeking a brighter, healthier future of recovery."

> **—Denise Bertin-Epp, RN, BScN, MSA**,
> president and CEO of the National Association for Children of Addiction (NACoA)

"Claudia Black has yet again created an indispensable resource for those in need of hope and recovery! As a person who entered long-term recovery as a teenager, as an addiction professional and, more importantly, as a father, I believe that Claudia has crafted a masterpiece that incorporates the critical elements a young person needs to identify the impact substance use is having on them and how to recover!"

— *Sean Walsh, LISAC*,
    CEO of Meadows Behavioral Healthcare

"Here's another masterpiece by Claudia Black. This trauma-informed workbook invites teens and young adults to explore their substance abuse and addiction. It features a treasure trove of clear and simple yet powerful activities, which allows them to be honest and more accountable for their behavior. Key tools and resources offer a path to living a life in recovery. This book is a game changer for youth."

— *Jerry Moe, MA*,
    National Director of Children's Programs, Emeritus, at Hazelden Betty Ford

"Claudia Black reaches out to teens to develop insight, to learn self-regulation, and to enhance life skills to support their life—now and in the future! Claudia's book, *Your Recovery, Your Life for Teens*, is a self-help book that tickles a teen's brain to move the teen to engage in critical thinking and support emotional intelligence. So necessary today!"

— *Cynthia Moreno Tuohy, BSW, NCACII, CDCIII, SAP*,
    author of *Rein in Your Brain*; and international, domestic, and local trainer

A TRAUMA-INFORMED WORKBOOK TO HELP YOU
HEAL FROM SUBSTANCE USE & ADDICTION

YOUR RECOVERY, YOUR LIFE
FOR TEENS

CLAUDIA BLACK, PHD

Instant Help Books

An Imprint of New Harbinger Publications, Inc.

Publisher's Note

This publication is designed to provide accurate and authoritative information in regard to the subject matter covered. It is sold with the understanding that the publisher is not engaged in rendering psychological, financial, legal, or other professional services. If expert assistance or counseling is needed, the services of a competent professional should be sought.

INSTANT HELP, the Clock Logo, and NEW HARBINGER are trademarks of New Harbinger Publications, Inc.

New Harbinger Publications is an employee-owned company.

Copyright © 2025 by Claudia Black
Instant Help Books
An imprint of New Harbinger Publications, Inc.
5720 Shattuck Avenue
Oakland, CA 94609
www.newharbinger.com

Cover design by Sara Christian

Interior design by Tom Comitta

Acquired by Georgia Kolias

Edited by Karen Levy

Library of Congress Cataloging-in-Publication Data on file

FSC
www.fsc.org
MIX
Paper | Supporting responsible forestry
FSC® C008955

Printed in the United States of America

27   26   25

10   9   8   7   6   5   4   3   2   1   First Printing

Dedicated to the many teens and young adults who have shared their journey with me and have been willing to take a look at the impact substances have had on your life. You've forever touched my heart.

CONTENTS

ACKNOWLEDGMENTS

John Meissbach, as I shared content, flow, and the exercises for *Your Recovery, Your Life* with you, your feedback was invaluable. Our process was fun and I so appreciated your youthful wisdom. Georgia Kolias, thank you for your perseverance and patience waiting for me to have open space in my life to bring this manuscript to fruition and for bringing me to New Harbinger Publications. Georgia Kolias and Vicraj Gill, I'm more than grateful for your guidance and collaboration throughout the development of this book. My longtime assistant, Sandi Klein, one more time you've kept me organized. Lastly, to the many young people who are willing to take a look at the impact substances are having in your life, know that I am with you in spirit.

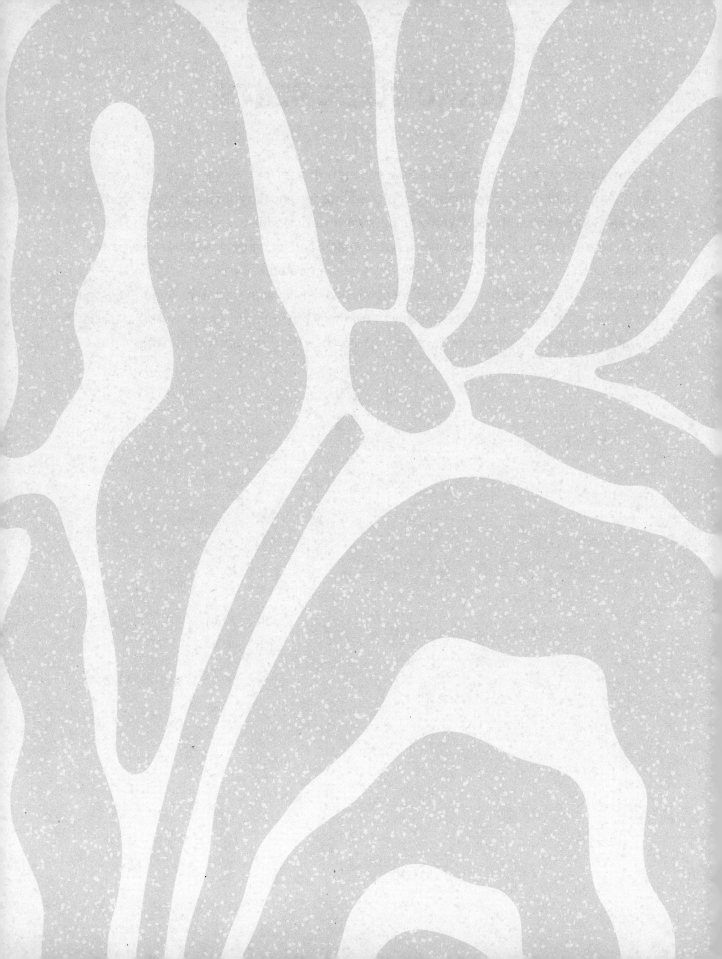

LETTER TO PARENTS

Dear Parent,

I appreciate your allowing me to be a part of your child's journey. By the time your young person needs to look at their use of substances, a lot has already taken place in the family. Chances are, you feel a bit of hope if your child has begun using this book, as an important step has taken place. At the same time, this frequently means there has been a history of fear, anger, maybe guilt, and a lot of confusion. Typically, these feelings have spread throughout the entire family, impacting you, other children, grandparents, stepparents, extended family members, and possibly even close family friends.

Experimenting with alcohol and drugs has historically been a rite of passage for our teenagers. It is not necessarily one we want for our children, but most people in Western society who will experience problems with drugs and alcohol start using between the ages of eleven and thirteen. But I doubt it is the experimenting that has you concerned. At the point a young person is being asked or asking for a workbook such as *Your Recovery, Your Life*, their use is already problematic. You may not know the seriousness of your child's use; you just know it is causing problems. And by the time you realize there could be a problem, it is usually more extensive than you thought. So, it's good that your child is exploring this now. It has the potential to make a wonderful difference in their life. If their choices and behavior regarding their use of substances are problematic to any degree, working with this book and making the choice to pursue recovery, a life not dictated by their use of substances, is an important step.

Young people who work with this book have varying motivations. Some already know they are in trouble and want help. Others are just trying to get parents or a judge or school counselor off their back. The idea of not using or drinking is often difficult for people of any age, and if that person is young, even more so. Our culture implies that using or drinking is symbolic of moving into adulthood, their peers may be using or drinking and they want to fit in, and social networks portray it as fun and the cool thing to do. Teenagers are at an age where they want independence and control over their own lives. Whatever your child's motivation for doing this workbook, the idea of stopping their substance use will be tough for them to accept. They don't want to be told what to do—and I am not going to do that. But I do hope to guide them through a process that allows them to be honest and more accountable for their behavior. This also means that this book is theirs to do—and your child will need some privacy in order to be willing to be honest and share openly. It is very likely they are doing this in the context of working with a counselor/therapist, and if so, that is where the work they do is best shared.

As a parent, reading this means you're taking your child's use of substances seriously, and that is to be commended, as many parents hope their child will simply grow out of this phase. You need to be their best parent, not their best friend, and that means you need to take their use seriously. Now is the time to learn about the young person's developing brain, substance addiction, and boundaries. Your child's recovery process will take time. During this time, you are still parenting them by helping them recognize choices and setting boundaries so that you and they know what is expected of them. Practicing non-enabling behavior is vital for your child's recovery.

I know this is a frightening and stressful time, so I encourage you to get support. Self-help groups, either in person or virtual, will welcome you and maintain your privacy around anything you share. Al-Anon, Nar-Anon, and PAL (Parents of Addicted Loved Ones) are programs for family members who are affected by someone else's use of alcohol or drugs. They will help lessen your sense of isolation and support you in healthy parenting. In addition, there are therapists and a variety of treatment resources with experience working with family members whose teens and young adults are struggling with substance use. Visit http://www.newharbinger. com/53356 for helpful websites. You don't need to walk this scary and confusing time alone.

Know that as your child makes their way through *Your Recovery, Your Life*, I am with you and your family in spirit.

LETTER TO READERS

ello,

I'm Claudia and I am hoping you will allow me to take you on a journey to look at what is happening in your life. I've struggled with some of the same things you are struggling with and, ultimately, I found my way by doing what you are doing: looking within myself. That led me to a career working with young people who struggle with feelings of depression and anxiety, often having experienced losses and maybe even trauma, and many have problems with their use of alcohol or other drugs. As I did, they too found their way, and so can you.

Some of you may have had your first experiences with substances as early as middle school, while others of you may not have started drinking or using until high school. It can get confusing as to what is normal and at what point your usage is getting you into trouble and you need to make some changes. You may or may not think you are in trouble; either way, this is an opportunity to get to know yourself better and look at the role substances play in your life. If not you, someone in your life feels you have a problem or you wouldn't be sitting with this book. Of course, if it wasn't your idea, that would also indicate you're probably not too happy about this. Ultimately, I ask that you stay open to what you can discover and make your own decisions. I'm here to help and guide you to look within and be the person you deserve to be, one who makes good decisions for yourself. The more honest you are, the more you will get out of *Your Recovery, Your Life*.

As I ask you to explore your use, I often refer to alcohol and other drugs as "mood-altering drugs" or "substances." This is because the possibilities are vast. Your experiences may be with one substance or many, and the substances in question could range from marijuana to alcohol, meth, cocaine, bath salts, ketamine, MDMA, heroin, fentanyl, oxycodone, Adderall, or Xanax. The number of substances out there is extensive. This book isn't about educating you on the harmful effects of drugs and alcohol; you can find that on the internet or in school programs. In this book, you will have the opportunity to learn about yourself and garner tools that will give you skills to better navigate your life. As you start reading, you will see that many exercises include some comments by other young people, and those are reflected in italics. Recognizing not all readers are still in their teenage years, I use the terms "teens" and "young people" interchangeably. Nonetheless, the message is meant for both teens and young adults. When parents are referred to, I am including all of the people who raised you. For some readers, this may be extended family members such as aunts and uncles or grandparents. Others may have been raised by caregivers such as those in the foster care system.

When I speak about recovery, I am speaking about the physical, emotional, social, and spiritual healing that can take place when you are no longer using alcohol and other drugs. Whether or not you are addicted is for you to answer. What is vital, though, is to get to a place of honesty so that you recognize the connection between your use of substances and your behavior. It will help you identify what you can do to change if your drinking or drugging is causing you problems. It will offer you the opportunity for insight and tools to identify your values, recognize your strengths, and pursue a life that brings you a sense of pride and self-respect. Today, there are tens of thousands of young people who are living wonderful lives after having stopped their use of substances and engaged in recovery practices. This workbook will help you get there.

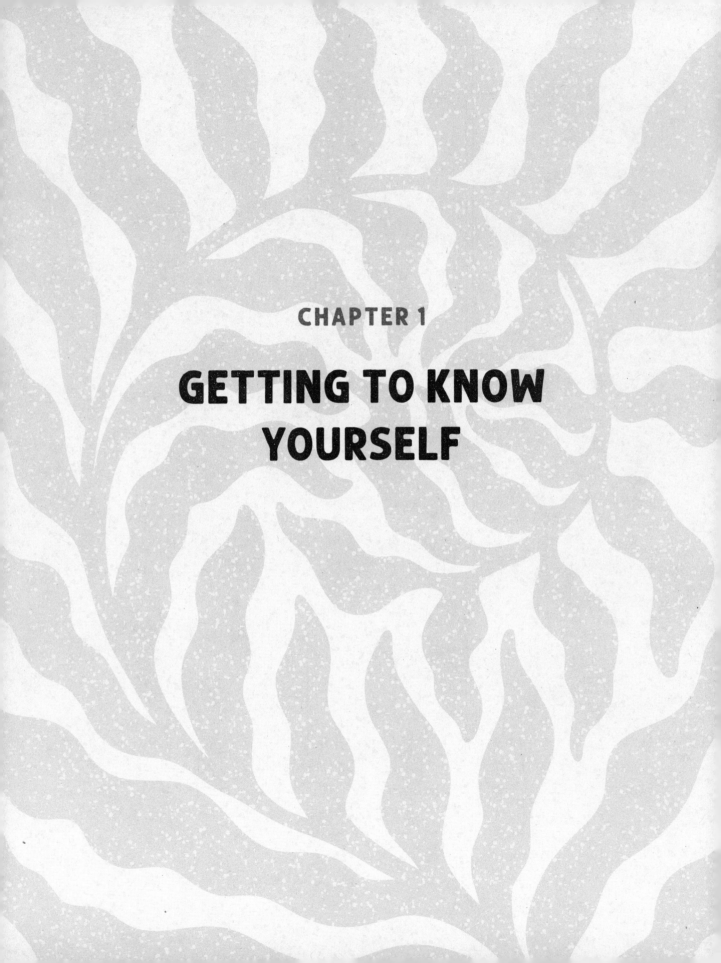

CHAPTER 1

GETTING TO KNOW YOURSELF

REFLECTING ON YOUR USE

Nearly everyone remembers the first time they used. Sometimes you remember because you got sick and needed to try and hide that from your parents so they wouldn't know the real reason you were throwing up or feeling so bad you couldn't get out of bed. Or you remember because you were with schoolmates or a family member, people who at the time were important to you, and it was a bonding experience. You felt part of a group; you felt seen. You may remember because for the first time in your life, you felt peace, as if an empty hole in your gut had been filled. Without even knowing anything was missing, you may have had a sense of "I have arrived," "This is amazing," or "This is what I have been waiting for."

Here are some comments other teens in recovery have made as they've learned to reflect on their use:

My friend texted me and told me to come over as his parents were gone and would be out late. We always liked it when our parents weren't home, as we would stay up late playing video games. But this time, when I got there, some other guys were there and they were all already using. They had pills, I think Oxy, and booze. I didn't want to act like a baby, and next thing I knew, I was really wasted. I barely remembered the night, but it was the beginning of lying to my parents about what I was doing.

I was twelve when I found some marijuana in my sister's room, so I got a few of my friends together after school and we all got high.

I was hanging around with this person that I really wanted to like me and he wanted me to use with him, so I did. I was afraid if I didn't, he'd dump me and date one of my other friends.

The first time I used, I was at camp and these older kids had a bunch of pills and alcohol. They pressured me to use with them, sort of like an initiation. I just wanted to be cool.

We had a family gathering and all of these cousins in their early twenties were there. They were all drinking, so I just poured myself a drink, too.

Reflecting on your first experience, describe the setting, your age, and what you were using.

_____

_____

_____

_____

When you are underage and know you could get into trouble for using, you still talk yourself into coming up with reasons it's okay to use or into thinking that you won't get caught. In the moment, the attraction to doing it is stronger than taking time out to think about not using. When that occurs, there is usually some self-talk that allowed you to go ahead and use.

What did you tell yourself about why it was okay? Circle any statements you identify with, and add any other self-talk you engaged in.

My friends are using and I want to be with them.

I'm old enough to make my own decisions.

No one will get hurt.

It's not really a drug.

I don't want to be the only one not using.

I want them to like me.

Self-talk is very subtle, and you often don't realize it is even occurring. While perhaps you didn't have a major conversation with yourself, be open to considering that there may have been unconscious or even conscious thoughts before you used, like Go ahead and do it. There may have also been thoughts after the experience that may have reinforced it, such as It was cool, These people are fun, or When is the next time I can do this?

What did you tell yourself about the first time you used?

_____

_____

_____

_____

Are you still telling yourself this?   **YES   NO**

If no, what is your self-talk today?

_____

_____

_____

_____

Give yourself a pat on the back for your willingness to think about these questions. Your experiences with substances and your self-talk are serious and hard for people of any age to explore. And when you're young, it's even more challenging. You may be thinking, "I've just started to live my life—I don't know if I want to give things up." For the moment, that is not the question or dictate. This book is only encouraging you to be honest with yourself.

AN OPPORTUNITY FOR HONESTY

People continue to use after their first time for lots of reasons. You may have had a good time under the influence: laughing, being silly, and joking with others. You may have felt the confidence to talk to someone you wanted to get to know. It may have lessened your inhibitions sexually, giving you courage to initiate or respond to someone. Or you may have felt a greater acceptance to be part of a certain group. Maybe you are stressed about school or have family issues. Many young people find substances take away a reality they don't like living in. But for just that moment, while under the influence, you aren't scared, lonely, hurt, or angry; it feels good. Or your use could be a combination of all those things.

Yet with continued use, negative consequences start to show. It's important that you stay aware of the impact of alcohol and other drugs on your life. All people who choose to use are at risk of experiencing problems. This is particularly true for young people.

Check the statements that apply to you. With my drinking and/or using:

☐   One drug has led me to use other drugs.

☐   I felt bad about myself, or guilty or ashamed because of something I did while under the influence.

☐   I didn't follow through with responsibilities.

☐   I said or did embarrassing things.

☐   My personality changes for the worse.

☐   I've done impulsive things or taken foolish risks.

☐   I've said cruel things to someone.

☐   I've lost friends.

☐   I no longer spend time with friends who don't use.

☐ I've broken or damaged property.

☐ I've had money problems (stole, or used money for substances and then couldn't pay other bills).

☐ Members of my family don't trust me.

☐ I've engaged in unsafe sex.

☐ Bad things happened to me.

☐ I've quit, been suspended, or fired from a job.

Sadly, the list of potential consequences can go on and on. *Are there other consequences you can think of that haven't been covered here?*

_____

_____

_____

Here is one teen's honest reflection of how her using had consequences for a friendship:

By 10th grade, I started hanging with these girls who were using and just ignored my best friend that I had had all through school. I ignored her texts, her phone calls. When I would see her, I would walk in a different direction. She didn't do anything wrong; she just didn't want to party like me. Then a few years later, she moved away, and I have never seen her again. I feel really bad about the way I treated her; she was a better friend than the other girls I was hanging around with. She really cared about me.

Of all the items you have checked or written down, circle three that concern you the most and explain why you chose those three consequences. *Describe what it is about these that feels the worst compared to the others.*

1. _____

_____

_____

2. _____

_____

_____

3. _____

_____

_____

Completing this activity is a big step. This is difficult work. It takes a lot of courage to say, "I have messed up" or "I have hurt others." Acknowledging your hurtful behavior likely doesn't make you feel good—but ignoring it only makes you feel worse about yourself. The good news is you don't have to continue to sabotage yourself or be hurtful to others. You can find ways to make up for your mistakes, understand what you truly value, and be who you truly want to be. For now, just the willingness to be honest with yourself is a start to feeling better about yourself.

RESPECTING THE BRAIN'S IMPACT

If you get honest, it's likely you did something you regret or you think of as stupid while under the influence. Perhaps you thought, "I won't do that again," and then you did it again. There is an explanation for that, and it has to do with your young brain.

Take a few moments to reflect on your last few experiences of using. Think about where you were, who you were with, what you were using, and what you thought about any consequences. As you reflect, don't rush; inhabit that past moment.

Now that you have a few scenes in mind from times you used, rate your capabilities on a scale of 1 to 10, with 1 being totally incapable to 10 being most capable of having the ability:

To make a healthy decision—one with your best interests at its core.

1   2   3   4   5   6   7   8   9   10

To think through a situation, identify your options, and make a good decision.

1   2   3   4   5   6   7   8   9   10

To behave the way you want to, without hurting yourself or others.

1   2   3   4   5   6   7   8   9   10

To recognize the possibility of consequences to your behavior.

1   2   3   4   5   6   7   8   9   10

To limit your use so you have control over your intentions.

1   2   3   4   5   6   7   8   9   10

What was it like completing this activity? Generally, substance use can compromise decision-making and problem-solving ability, judgment, and self-control.

Right now, you're between being a teenager and an adult. There are a lot of physiological and psychological changes you're adjusting to. You're at a pivotal stage where you're considering your future—what you value and what is important to you. And while that is happening, your brain is still developing. You're inclined toward high excitement; you're less likely to consider potential negative outcomes before you act. Don't take this as a personal insult or some kind of flaw unique to you; it reflects the state of your brain.

In your brain, there's a region called the prefrontal cortex (PFC). It's the brain's thinking center, responsible for decision making, problem solving, self-control, and judgment. It also won't fully develop until your mid-twenties. What often rules our world until the PFC is fully developed is our midbrain, tucked behind and under the PFC. Here is the limbic system, the part of our brain that regulates drives and instincts. Inside that limbic system is a structure called the amygdala. The amygdala helps you react to threats, something that was necessary in our ancient past. But the threats we face now aren't predators on the savannah; they're tests, surprise assignments, or friends we fear might judge us, for example. The amygdala reacts to these events in ways that spur us to use less of our thinking skills (which we need) and more of our reacting skills (which are often not so helpful). That reinforces impulsivity and lack of judgment.

Your teenage brain is also being driven by a chemical known as dopamine. Dopamine is the predominant chemical in our brain that allows us to experience pleasure; it also reinforces our continued use of what makes us feel good. When substances enter the brain, the brain releases an excessive amount of dopamine, overloading the body with pleasurable feelings. The brain is wired to feel as though these pleasurable activities are life-sustaining, that we need them. We want more.

At this time in your life, your dopamine levels are at their highest level. You have so many dopamine sensors that experiences can feel truly awesome. And you seek out experiences that make you feel good. This can set you up for risk. You also get a bigger hit of dopamine when you do new things. And that means you get less reinforcement—less feel-good energy—for the routine, often boring tasks that you may need to do, such as homework.

This means that no matter how smart or talented you are, your ability to use judgment, have self-control, be a problem solver, and make good decisions will be limited until you are at least in your mid-twenties. And all of this is occurring while you are being granted more adult opportunities—such as getting a driver's license or a job—and making decisions about work, school, careers, and relationships. No wonder this is often a confusing time. Your brain is incredibly vulnerable and seriously powerful. And that's a tricky combination. It's why you have moments of unbelievable insight and experiences where you act in ways you almost immediately regret. Growth and chaos often exist simultaneously.

Add to all this the impact substances can have. When you're using, you're less likely to be able to tap into your PFC, which is at serious risk of being hijacked by the limbic system, which is driven by excitement. For instance, your limbic system might tell you something like, "Let's break into this house and get a few things—no one will see us," and even if your PFC kicks in ("That's not a good idea, and that stuff doesn't belong to us"), your limbic system and amygdala might win out—especially if you're using substances. And again, substances also increase dopamine levels. When something in our brain allows us to feel a high amount of pleasure, the brain considers that an important activity: "I like it, let's do it again, again, and again." That is where the risk of using comes into play.

See if you can come up with at least three examples of this sentence: "My limbic system was in control when I..." *What behaviors did your limbic system and amygdala drive you to do—even if part of you didn't want to, or knew better?*

Other teens in recovery have said their limbic system told them:

It was okay to jump in front of cars on the freeway.

It was okay to start taking meth.

It was okay to forget what my parents told me about using drugs.

1. My limbic system was in control when I

   _____

   _____

2. My limbic system was in control when I

   _____

   _____

3. My limbic system was in control when I

   _____

   _____

Brain science isn't an excuse for behavior that's illegal, unwise, or impulsive. It's an explanation. Having a good time, having fun, and feeling pleasure are all important parts of life. But if you're at the point that chasing the good times is causing chaos and bad times, then you won't reap the benefits of fulfilling your dreams and goals.

You don't have to wait until you're older to be in charge of your life. Your brain, like all brains, is moldable. It can be changed by experience; it can be changed when you behave differently. In fact, your young brain has the advantage of being extremely capable of learning new things. Much of this book is designed to help you harness this capacity: to teach you ways to use your PFC to calm down the reactivity of the amygdala and limbic system.

NOTICING THE INFLUENCES

Anyone who uses alcohol and other drugs has the potential to develop a substance use problem. However, some people are at greater risk of developing these problems than others. It is very easy to think and even say that this is what teenagers and young adults do, but it isn't as simple as that. Everyone is influenced by outside forces, particularly as they are growing up. In this exercise, you'll think about which forces, ranging from psychological, social, cultural, sexuality and gender, and biological, have influenced you. While they are not excuses, this reflection will help you identify any vulnerabilities you have that drive your substance use, giving you the chance to lessen the more negative influences while enhancing the more constructive ones. Ultimately, this is all a part of feeling your inner strength.

Psychological Influences

The use of alcohol and or other drugs is often an answer when we don't feel good about ourselves or when we lack confidence. When under the influence, it's easier to forget about our problems or act in ways that are outside of our norm. Sometimes this allows us to get more acceptance from others or attention for ourselves. If we are struggling with any type of anxiety or depression, substances can temporarily relieve us of our fears or numb our emotional pain. It becomes a temporary solution to a problem.

Circle or highlight the statements you identify with. Have you used alcohol or other drugs...

To help you feel more confident?

To help you overcome being nervous or anxious?

To help you deal with boredom?

To help get you out of depressed thoughts?

Social Influences

As social creatures, we want a sense of belonging and connection with others. If others that we look up to and want acknowledgment from are using, be it friends or family, we often use to be able to fit in or feel we belong with them. They may encourage us or even make fun of us if we don't.

Circle or highlight the statements you identify with. Is your use motivated by...

Wanting acceptance by others you admire or want acknowledgment from

Wanting to be seen as cool or popular

Wanting to feel more at ease around others

Wanting to pursue or engage in romantic interests

Having peers encourage it

Having family members model or encourage you

Cultural Influences

Culture involves many forces. Everyone is influenced by religion and ethnicity. You are influenced by messages you hear via the internet, social media, videos, and what you read. You have also grown up in an era with a greater likelihood of shootings in your community or school and greater violence throughout the country, which previous generations have not experienced.

SCREEN USE

The experience of FOMO, the fear of missing out, fuels a lot of anxiety and depression. You may spend hours on your phone or the internet following threads that show someone you admire or want to be like living the good life. This person appears to be having all the fun—romance, sex, drinking, drugging, and having money. They don't look lonely, afraid, or sad. It's enticing. You might drink or drug, thinking that you too will have the life this person is projecting. Or because your life doesn't look the way this person's does, you use in response to the despair you feel. The impact of the internet also fuels an expectation of quick fixes or immediate answers, which gets in the way of being patient and accepting that the rewards of effort and hard work, which so many things in life require, take time.

Are you spending time on social media sites that reinforce using or drinking?　　YES　NO

If you answered yes, explain.

_____

_____

_____

Do you think FOMO reinforces your using?　　YES　NO

If you answered yes, explain.

_____

_____

_____

Think about the music, videos, and posts that you encounter. Are you hearing messages that reinforce using?　　YES　NO

If you answered yes, explain.

_____

_____

_____

RELIGIOUS AND ETHNIC INFLUENCES

Many religions don't reinforce using drugs and may accept only moderate use of substances like alcohol or encourage abstinence altogether. If religious beliefs are a part of your life, and you choose to use, you may need to be secretive with your use, or you may believe your use is shameful. On the other hand, it may be possible your using is a way of rebelling against something you don't enjoy or agree with in a way you cannot express otherwise.

As with religion, your ethnic history may also influence your using practices. Some ethnic cultures reinforce drinking at a young age and encourage it as central to social and familial gatherings. Other ethnic populations have strict laws against any use of alcohol as well as other drugs to the extent of it being criminal. When culture is restrictive and there is no modeling for moderation, and if this has passed through the generations, your biology may not have the tolerance that others have, creating a quick escalation into out-of-control drinking and using.

Do you think religion or ethnicity has influenced your use of drugs or alcohol? **YES NO**

If you answered yes, explain.

_____

_____

_____

Sexuality and Gender

Young people struggling with their sexual orientation or gender identity are much more likely to use drugs and alcohol at an earlier age and as a consequence struggle with substance use disorders. You are at an age where you are recognizing your gender and sexual identity and you may be struggling with the certainty of your feelings. You may be confused about who you can talk to. You may fear rejection from family, friends, and people throughout your school and community. You may even experience hate from strangers.

Do you think your confusion or identification with gender or sexual orientation   **YES NO**
influences your use of alcohol and drugs?

If you answered yes, explain.

_____

_____

_____

_____

Biological Influences

While some children raised with parental substance addiction choose not to drink because of what they have witnessed, most children ultimately make the decision to drink or use a drug their parent was not addicted to. In doing so, they often believe they will have the willpower to control their use and not end up like their parents. Yet willpower doesn't prevent addiction. If you are the biological child of someone addicted to substances, you may be at greater risk of developing problems based on your genetic makeup. The results of biological studies indicate that children of parents who are addicted to alcohol and other drugs react differently to substances.

It is important to know that it is the biological vulnerability that is inherited, not necessarily the addiction. That means you are more prone to becoming addicted if you start using; it does not mean you will become addicted.

Nonetheless, this biological predisposition needs to be taken seriously. And if you add any type of psychological pain or additional influences like the ones we discuss in this section, the likelihood of becoming addicted substantially increases.

Is there anyone in your family you think has or had a problem with their use of drugs or alcohol?   **YES NO**

If you don't know, consider asking another family member. It's possible a relative has not been identified or referred to as alcoholic or an addict but you heard stories or witnessed their excessive and possibly hurtful use of alcohol or drugs. Sometimes addiction can skip a generation. It's also true that you may be part of a family in which the parents don't drink at all, or drink very little, yet one or more of the children, possibly you, may not be able to drink without it being a problem.

Some of you already know you have a parent who is alcoholic or addicted and you may have vowed to yourself that this will never happen to you and you will not become like them. Whatever your situation, it's crucial to understand you are not your parent (or other caregiver). It's possible you may become addicted as your parent is or was, but that may be only one commonality; you can choose to be quite different than them in recovery.

Now that you have had an opportunity to consider five predominant influences, circle the dynamics that you think have an impact on you.

Psychological   Sexuality and gender

Social   Biological

Cultural

Knowing about these influences may help you make decisions about your use. And it can give you direction for taking specific actions to support a healthy lifestyle for yourself.

WHEN SUBSTANCES TAKE THE LEAD

Imagine you are in a horse race. You are initially the horse out in front, but in time, and sometimes it doesn't take long, the horse called Substance passes by and takes the lead, dictating your path. You make attempts at getting back in front, and may even get ahead every once in a while, but ultimately Substance takes the lead. Being faster and stronger, Substance stays there. In these moments, we're effectively powerless against the substances we've come to rely on. Remember that substances dampen the activity of our PFC, our ability to think through situations, making it a lot easier to default to impulsive behavior or not recognize the consequences of the impulsive behavior. None of us likes to think of ourselves as powerless, which we equate with defeat, with losing. But when it comes to using substances, the nature of how it works in the brain often leads to having an overpowering grip on our thinking, behaviors, and decisions.

See if any of the following facets of powerlessness resonate for you. I've included some thoughts on powerlessness that other teens have had as well.

- Powerlessness is when drinking or using is causing you problems, yet you continue.

  I am not powerless; using before school is just something I do. I like getting high before my first class.

  Even after I got kicked out of school for drinking, I didn't stop. The teachers just had it out for me.

  I got caught by my mom a few times for drinking, so I just knew I had to be more careful.

- Powerlessness is when the urge to use alcohol or other drugs becomes more important than school, family, old friends, or other activities.

    When my good friends started to challenge me about my using, I just decided I didn't need them in my life and found myself hanging out with the kids who were using like me.

    When I found myself missing out on my music classes because I preferred to be out using, I just told myself I wasn't that good enough at it anyway, so it was no loss.

- Powerlessness is when life begins to unravel and you feel out of control.

    Once I start to get high, I stay high until my supply and my money are gone. Then I start to strategize who I can go use with or steal from.

Which statements about powerlessness resonate for you and why?

_____

_____

_____

A hard fact of life is that there will be many things that you don't have power over, but you do have power over the choices you make. A part of recovery is owning the power you have, and it begins with honesty about what is currently happening in your life around your drinking and using. Some signs that alcohol or drug use is a driving force in your life are 1) a preoccupation with using, 2) a loss of control when using, 3) attempts to stop that have not been successful, and 4) negative consequences from using. Let's explore how these factors might be influencing your use of alcohol and drugs. I've included other teens' experiences as well.

Preoccupation

I was driving and got in an accident because I was texting my dealer and strategizing how we were going to link up.

Describe two times when you were thinking about using or how you were going to acquire the substances when you were supposed to be focused on something else.

1. _____

   _____

   _____

2. _____

   _____

   _____

Loss of Control

I was going home for the holiday and told myself I would only drink beer at my parents' house. The next thing I knew, I'd gone into their pantry and stolen a bottle of vodka.

There have probably been times when you used or drank more than you had intended and your drive to use became more powerful than your plan or intentions. **Describe a situation when you drank or used more than you planned to.**

_____

_____

_____

Attempts to Stop

I told myself I'd give up the Oxy, but I could still drink, and after two drinks, I was back taking the Oxy even more than when I first quit.

Sometimes you may recognize that you needed to lessen or even stop your using to feel more in control, but if you are in trouble, that is short-lived, and in a matter of time you are back to your regular use, or using even more, or you've switched your drug of choice. This, too, is an expression of a fundamental powerlessness.

Describe a time when you recognized the need to lighten up or even stop, or maybe you switched to another drug of choice to lessen the negative impact, but it didn't work; in spite of your best intentions, you went back to what you were doing and maybe began using or drinking more.

_____

_____

_____

_____

Negative Consequences

Instead of studying for my college entrance exam, I was getting high all the time and now I can't get into a four-year school.

Ongoing use of substances often leads to negative consequences. You may have already experienced some losses due to your drinking and using behaviors. Perhaps others don't realize why you've experienced these losses, but when you're honest with yourself, you can see your use of substances was connected.

Circle or highlight the losses you have experienced as a result of your drinking or using. Add your own to the list.

Family member's trust

A romantic partner

Job

Money

Educational opportunities

Good grades

Athletic opportunity

Reputation

Self-respect

Clean legal record

Time

Driving privileges

Car or other property

Other: _____

Other: _____

Pick three of the items you lost due to your use of alcohol and drugs and describe the impact that has had on you.

1. _____

_____

_____

2. _____

_____

_____

3. _____

_____

_____

Acknowledging that your use of alcohol and or other drugs has gotten in front of you and that substances are leading the race can be tough. But it's also a way of taking back your power. In essence, the ability to recognize where you have power and where you don't gives you a new freedom.

WHEN LIFE BECOMES MESSY

If you are having a problem with alcohol or drugs, chances are, your life is not going too smoothly. Does it seem like things at home, work, or school are getting messy? Is your relationship with your girl/boyfriend becoming too complicated? Are things you were planning just not working out like you wanted? Perhaps it feels like the universe is aligned against you. When your parents, siblings, or friends try to give you some advice or direction, do you find yourself angry or resentful toward them for intruding?

When life isn't working out the way you want, it's often easier to start to ignore the problem areas and cling to the parts that seem to bring you some comfort, such as alcohol and drugs. But this also has a way of escalating the problems you're facing, rather than helping you deal with them. In this activity, you are asked to take an honest look at how substance use is impacting you. The following questions require a lot of honesty to be helpful. Others may not recognize the changes in you, or attribute them to your using, but this is for you, not someone else.

How Is School Going?

Describe how your performance at work or school is going or has changed over time due to your use.

_____

_____

_____

_____

Been in Any Risky or Dangerous Situations?

When underage and drinking or using, it's easy to find yourself in some high-risk situations where you are no longer safe. You may have been in danger or in legal trouble as a result of who you were associating with, your location, or the extent of your drinking or using. One of the most common high-risk situations is sexual assault, and that is true across genders. When under the influence, you may not be able to protect yourself, you may not be able to flee a situation, or you may be incapacitated.

Does any of this ring true? (I am not going to ask you to write about it, but I want you to answer.) YES NO

Have you found yourself in any compromising situations that nearly or did get you into legal trouble? YES NO

Were there times you felt peer pressure to use a drug that you felt was too dangerous or drink more than you wanted? YES NO

Have you ever stolen alcohol or drugs or items to be able to buy alcohol and other drugs? YES NO

Have you broken into any places to acquire substances, or to have an isolated place to use or just crash? YES NO

Engaging in Any Self-Harm and Harm to Others?

Not only can substance use lead us to put ourselves in risky situations, but it can also drive us to harm ourselves or others, even if that isn't what we intended.

Describe a time when you got hurt or someone else got hurt because of things you did while drinking or high.

_____

_____

_____

_____

Sometimes you could be in a situation that turned out okay, but perhaps that was more luck than anything. For instance, perhaps you were loaded behind the wheel with a friend and had a car accident; the two of you ended up with just minor injuries, but it could easily have been worse, and the people with or around you could've been badly hurt, too. That's a situation of hurting yourself and nearly hurting someone else. Or say you were babysitting your younger sister and you took her with you while you went to score. Again, perhaps nothing happened—but something easily could have.

Describe a time that your using or drinking put another person in jeopardy.

_____

_____

_____

_____

Have you ever used or drank so much you don't remember your actions? Perhaps sometimes you laugh about that, but other times, you have this sense of dread. Either way, this too is an example of not being in control.

Describe a time someone told you about something you did when under the influence and you have no memory of that.

_____

_____

_____

_____

Sometimes, experiences like these can leave you with something called moral injury. This is the feeling you get when you've done something or experienced something that violates your morals or conscience. It often results in intense feelings of guilt, shame, or even anger. If these are feelings you're struggling with, know that chapter 2 will cover some skills to help you process these feelings and work with them in ways that are constructive and not destructive.

How's It Going with Family?

Chances are your parents may not be too happy about your using and drinking, and it's also very likely they don't know the extent of it.

Whether or not your parents understand that your behavior is connected to your use of substances, how do you think your relationship has changed with anyone in your family due to your using and drinking?

_____

_____

_____

_____

How Is It Going with Friends?

Have any of your relationships changed with friends due to your using and drinking?

_____

_____

_____

_____

Thank you for your willingness to answer these tough questions, or at least consider them. The answers don't always make us feel good. In fact, that is why we make excuses, lie, or simply ignore thinking about things like this. And when your behavior is hurtful to yourself or others, you can do something about that. That's the intent of doing this workbook—to think about your behavior and whether you want to make some new decisions for yourself.

STRENGTHS FOR DOING IT DIFFERENTLY

No matter how much trouble you may be experiencing, or how hopeless or angry you may feel, now is the time to take inventory of your strengths and things you value that can carry you forward.

All of us are good at listing what we don't like about ourselves, but our strengths outweigh our vulnerabilities. So set aside any negative thoughts. It is these strengths that will help you make the changes you decide to make.

Below, you'll see a set of words for different strengths we can have. *Circle any of these traits that you have demonstrated at some time in your life.* It doesn't matter if it has not been in the recent past, just that you have demonstrated it at some time.

Willing	Trusting	Trustworthy	Thorough
Resourceful	Reliable	Patient	Reasonable
Organized	Loving	Smart	Honest
Hardworking	Focused	Energetic	Eager
Flexible	Determined	Creative	Confident
Careful	Brave	Adventurous	Unique
Social	Consistent	Open-minded	Artistic
Kind	Athletic	Graceful	

Now, take five of the strengths that you most identify with and describe a time in which you showed this strength.

EXAMPLES:

Smart: I can solve the Rubik's Cube.

Kind: I am kind to animals.

Athletic: I can run a mile.

STRENGTH 1. _____

STRENGTH 2. _____

STRENGTH 3. _____

STRENGTH 4. _____

STRENGTH 5. _____

While everyone has strengths, your strengths help define you, and they set you apart from others. They are what make you uniquely you. Even if you don't feel or act on them all the time, or it's been a long time since you demonstrated these characteristics, allow yourself to acknowledge these are parts of who you are. For this moment, hold on to that.

Another fun way to acknowledge yourself is by thinking of positive attributes and strengths and applying them to each letter of your name.

Write your name with space to add positive attributes and strengths to each letter.

You may not feel these attributes describe you most recently. Or perhaps you've used some of your strengths recently—and it is also possible you used them in a way that wasn't in your best interest—but if the attribute is there, within you, it can be tapped into and used in a positive manner. You have it; now it's time to use it more in your life, and to use it to the ends that will truly serve you.

MOVING FORWARD

You're doing well: you got through this first chapter. Feel good about it. As much as you might like to have your troubles behind you, recovery is a process, and if you can acknowledge your progress, it allows you to be more accepting that this takes time. Thinking about change, when things are not going well, is one thing; starting to make changes is another step. But you've been contemplating what's happening in your life, and change has begun with your willingness to do this work.

This grounding practice can be especially helpful when you feel overwhelmed by whirling thoughts or strong feelings.

GROUNDING: DEEP BREATHING

1. Stand up and place your feet shoulder-width apart so you are stable.

2. Take a few deep breaths.

3. Relax your shoulders and drop your hands to your sides. Let your arms and hands dangle.

4. Take in a long, deep breath through your nose, then blow it out through your mouth like a big gust of wind. Try to breathe from your abdomen, not your chest.

5. Repeat step 4 several times.

CHAPTER 2

NAME THAT FEELING

GETTING TO KNOW YOUR FEELINGS

Apart of the human condition is the emotional self, expressed with feelings. Feelings can be both pleasurable and painful, but we all have them. When we listen to them, they will tell us something important about ourselves and can direct us toward self-care, getting support, and possibly doing some problem solving.

The following is a list of feelings; *add any you can think of not on the list.*

Love	Hurt	Fear	Hate
Worry	Shame	Anger	Guilt
Sadness	Brave	Jealousy	Joy
Resentment	Happy	Frustration	Embarrassment
Lonely	Hopeful	Disappointment	Hopeless
Discouraged	Encouraged	Caring	Excited
Confused	Anxious		

We often have more than one feeling at a time, and those feelings may seem contrary to each other. We can love and hate, be sad and angry, or feel fearful and happy at the same time. We also experience feelings with different levels of intensity, from mild to very intense. The ability to identify what you are feeling and its intensity is the first step to managing your emotions.

When we were toddlers and young children, we were spontaneous with our feelings. But by the time we become teenagers, we have received a lot of messages about what is and what is not okay to feel. If you were lucky, you heard messages that helped you recognize what you were feeling and those feelings were honored—messages like, "I am so sorry you are hurting," "I know that was frustrating," and "I've been embarrassed, too." But often, the messages we got were more like, "You have nothing to be angry about," "That wasn't embarrassing," and "Boys don't cry." We may have heard these messages from family members, friends, or other adults and through the media. What's more, the older we get, the less spontaneous we tend to be about showing people what we feel. Instead, we tend to present what we think others want to see or what has been modeled for us.

Beliefs that shut us down emotionally include:

People will take advantage of you if you show your feelings.

There is no point in showing your feelings; no one will be there for you anyway.

I am the only one who feels this way.

Other people have it worse than me, so why should I feel this way?

Toughen up, don't be weak.

We mask feelings we don't want other people to know about. For example, some of us may mask sadness with humor, fear with intellectualizing, or anger with a smile. Or we might mask one feeling with another, such as masking anger with sadness, or using anger to mask feeling fearful.

What feelings are you masking? When you are masking a feeling, there is something that tells you that certain feelings you're having—anger, sadness, fear, anxiety, insecurity—are not okay to share.

1. *Identify three feelings you have difficulty letting other people see.*

2. *Note what mask you use to hide the real feeling.*

3. *Identify the fear that makes you want to put the mask on.* Do you fear you might be judged, or that you won't be understood? Do you fear that if you express your true feelings, you'll lose control? Or perhaps you fear you are being disloyal to someone important to you. It is possible that at some point you were told that it wasn't okay to feel as you do. Whatever your fear, it doesn't have to make sense. It just is. Write the first thing that comes to mind.

EXAMPLES:

If I were to show my sadness, I fear you would look at me strange and walk away.

If I were to show my anger, I fear you would not want to be my friend.

FEELING: _____

MASK: _____

FEAR: _____

FEELING: _____

MASK: _____

FEAR: _____

FEELING: _____

MASK: _____

FEAR: _____

Keep in mind that the fears we have about expressing our feelings are usually based in some reality. Maybe someone tried to take that feeling away from you by saying you were wrong to feel that way, or you received no support or compassion for how you were feeling. Often a show of feelings can be met with disapproval, shaming messages, rejection, or even punishment. When you see it in this light, masking is a way of protecting yourself.

We trust some people more than others and are therefore more apt to let them know how we feel. Then again, sometimes we don't want to disappoint those we care about the most, so we may do the opposite and not let them know what we are feeling. Wanting acceptance, be it from a family member or a friend, we may share some feelings but not others. All of that is understandable.

What did you learn about feelings that is important for you to remember?

_____

_____

_____

DIFFICULT FEELINGS: FEAR

We all have fears, even when we present as happy and confident. Some of us know how to cope with our fears; it is also possible we hide them and try to run from them. We often keep our fears a secret because we are embarrassed or have been told that being afraid is a sign of weakness. But fear will only grow stronger if it is locked up inside. It will fuel our imagination and drive our behaviors in ways we can't control, unless we learn to recognize and work with it.

We don't always think of ourselves as being afraid or in fear, but there are many other words on the continuum of experiencing fear that you may identify with.

Afraid	Anxious	Stressed
Intimidated	Vulnerable	Insecure
Terrified	Panicky	Threatened
Tormented	Frantic	Overwhelmed
Tense	Full of dread	

Here are some thoughts other teens in recovery have had about fear:

I was afraid no one would like me.

I was afraid my dad wouldn't come home. I was afraid when he did.

I was afraid I would fail at most things I tried.

I was afraid to let anyone see I was afraid.

Identify three of these fear feelings that you've experienced.

1. _____

2. _____

3. _____

If you acknowledged any of these fears, did you let anyone else know what you were feeling? If so, describe who you shared it with and their response.

_____

_____

_____

On a scale of 1 to 10, where 1 is not at all and 10 is all the time, to what degree has fear been a part of your life?

1   2   3   4   5   6   7   8   9   10

Check the statement that best describes the relationship between your fear and your use of substances.

☐   When I use, it helps me not to feel any fear.

☐   I use my fear as an excuse to get loaded or high.

☐   When I use, I don't care so much about things that have caused me fear.

On a scale of 1 to 10, where 1 is not at all and 10 is definitely, how likely is it that you used alcohol and drugs to anesthetize or cope with fear?

1   2   3   4   5   6   7   8   9   10

The reality is you cannot get through life without being scared, so the goal isn't to never be scared. The goal is to know when you feel fear and not medicate it with substances. When you're able to recognize your fear, rather than resisting it, you can even tap into how the fear might be helpful. At its core, fear is a feeling like any other—and all our feelings serve as sources of information. They tell us about the situations we're in, and about our needs within those situations. If we can be mindful of our feelings, willing to acknowledge them rather than masking them, we can become more aware of what we need and how to get it. Here are some ways to cope when fear arises.

- Breathe. Just stop and take a breath. Pause, take another breath. Slow down, and breathe—in to the count of four, out to the count of five. Repeat the cycle at least four times.

- Ask yourself, "How can I let this fear help me? What needs might the fear be pointing me toward?"

- Say the following out loud, completing the sentence. Say it slowly and repeat five times: "I am scared and it would be good for me to _____."

- Journal about your fear.

- Share it with someone.

- Get more information about what frightens you.

- Name the emotion and change the self-talk. We often make assumptions and see only the worst possibility when we are afraid, so we catastrophize, then react. For instance, say you're afraid you'll lose your job because you're late—so you tell yourself, "Don't even bother to go to work." Instead of being afraid and thinking you're doomed, pause again, and remind yourself that this may not be true. You are only assuming you will get fired; you don't know that. Often, fear and negative thoughts can take root and distort the severity of the situation. Stop and ask, "What's another possibility? Am I taking all the factors of this situation into account? Is the fear I feel distorting my thinking?"

- Consider: Will the fearful thoughts you're having solve your problem or help you reach your goals?

- Consider: Who in your life can help you think this through?

- Exercise can boost your mood and calm your mind.

Here are some things other kids in recovery have come to discover when they've learned how to work with their fears.

Today when I get scared, I tell myself to stop and breathe. And count slowly to ten. Then, I tell myself fear is just a feeling, and that's all it is. It is telling me I need to ask what is the best way to take care of myself right now.

My self-talk can kill me or make me. So now, instead of putting myself down or blaming someone when I am scared, I ask myself: How realistic is this? Whom can I share it with? Today I have people who are safe for me to talk to.

DIFFICULT FEELINGS: LONELINESS

Sometimes young people feel very lonely. It may have begun when you were so young that being alone is a comfortable place, and you don't risk any rejection. Maybe you spend a lot of time just walking, ambling about the neighborhood, or isolating in your room with a television, an iPad, or a computer. You may have become resourceful and developed hobbies you can engage in on your own. Or perhaps you assuaged the loneliness by finding virtual friends through gaming or social media. Gaming can offer a sense of belonging and being part of something; social media is also a way to feel some level of connection. The connections you make on platforms are literally "friends," and you're engaged in liking and commenting on each other's posts or other activities. But perhaps when you take the devices away, you are still left with that loneliness.

Here are some thoughts other teens in recovery have had about loneliness:

I have always felt like I am on the outside looking in.

For the most part, I feel like I am not seen.

No one cares.

I'm not good enough for them (friends, classmates, family).

Where do you find yourself feeling lonely? School? Work? Home? Certain times of the day? All the time? Everywhere? Describe it here.

_____

_____

_____

_____

On a scale of 1 to 10, where 1 is not at all and 10 is all the time, to what degree has loneliness been a part of your life?

1   2   3   4   5   6   7   8   9   10

Using is also, often, a way to connect with others, to be a part of a group or certain social circle. It may be a way to get attention from others. In the moment you don't feel so alone.

Circle or highlight the statement that best describes the relationship between your loneliness and your substance use.

When I use, I don't feel so alone.

When I use, it numbs that pain of loneliness.

I use to make friends.

On a scale of 1 to 10, where 1 is not at all and 10 is definitely, how likely is it you use alcohol or drugs to anesthetize or cope with loneliness?

1   2   3   4   5   6   7   8   9   10

While loneliness may actually fuel your desire to use substances, choosing to not drink or use can fuel the fear of loneliness. You may be asking, "Will others want me to be around them if I am not using with them?" While that is a common fear among young people, it is possible to find ways to not feel lonely when alone and find connection with others who can support you in a recovery process. The following are options that you may find helpful.

- Engage in a creative activity you enjoy. It may be creative writing, playing an instrument, or drawing. Art is fundamentally a form of communication. You may be alone doing it, but you won't feel the loneliness.

- Practice an act of kindness. It's another way to establish contact with those around you. When at a store, offer to carry the bags for someone who appears to be struggling. Or if you're in a line, let another person go ahead of you. Offer a ride to someone who needs one. Extend yourself to be available to others in need.

- On a weekly basis, plan to get together with someone. Knowing you have a plan to connect can assuage the immediate sense of aloneness.

- Join a group. This could be a class at a community college, the gym, or a self-help group.

- Make eye contact when you speak to someone. This facilitates better connection.

Here are some things other kids in recovery have realized help them no longer feel lonely.

I call my friends in recovery and we talk or get together and hang out.

First and foremost, I own it. I recognize it for what it is.

I remind myself about my own goals and how I am making good decisions for myself.

I remind myself how well I am doing in recovery. This doesn't always take away all the loneliness, but lessens it.

DIFFICULT FEELINGS: SADNESS

People feel sad for many reasons. You may feel sad when you miss someone you love or care about, when you feel like you don't fit in, or when troubling things happen to you.

Here are some thoughts other teens in recovery have had about sadness:

I cry myself to sleep a lot, but no one knows.

I wish my mom or dad knew how I felt inside.

I hate feeling sad.

On a scale of 1 to 10, where 1 is not at all and 10 is all the time, to what degree has sadness been a part of your life?

1   2   3   4   5   6   7   8   9   10

The natural desire when you're feeling sad is to be comforted by someone, you don't feel alone in your pain or can have your pain validated. Yet, as we grow older, we often take on beliefs that tell us others don't want to be around us if we're sad. It's very likely that you hide your pain.

Identify three situations in which you felt sad. If you expressed it outwardly, describe how: Did you cry? Share your sadness with someone? Try to ignore it in some way?

I felt sad when: _____

I expressed it by: _____

I felt sad when: _____

I expressed it by: _____

I felt sad when: _____

I expressed it by: _____

If you don't like others to know you feel sad, when was the last time you showed your sadness to someone? How old were you? How did the people around you respond? What did you tell yourself about being sad or expressing it after that?

_____

_____

_____

_____

Check the statement that best describes the relationship between your sadness and use of substances.

- ☐ When I use, it helps me to not feel my sadness.

- ☐ I use my sadness as an excuse to get high.

- ☐ When I use, I don't care about things that have caused me sadness.

On a scale of 1 to 10, where 1 is not at all and 10 is definitely, how likely is it you used alcohol and drugs to anesthetize or cope with sadness?

1 2 3 4 5 6 7 8 9 10

By the time you are a teenager, there are many things that can bring on sadness: your parents divorcing, a caregiver not showing up for you the way you want, the loss of a pet, the loss of a family member, the loss of an opportunity to be in a school event or sport, or the loss when you change schools or a good friend moves away.

You have reasons for all of your feelings, and they often fuse with each other. To feel a chronic sense of sadness, for instance, can lead to loneliness, which can lead to fear, which can then lead to anger. Then you feel guilty about all of that.

The first step, often, is to separate the feelings out—to understand exactly what you're feeling, and what might be driving that. Ultimately, there are ways to cope with each feeling you experience, and once you have a sense of what's going on for you, you can use some of these coping strategies. ***Check the ones you are willing to try.***

- ☐ Acknowledge there are reasons for your sadness.

- ☐ Be kind and compassionate with yourself.

- ☐ Remind yourself that all feelings pass, and this feeling will too.

- ☐ Make connections with others.

- ☐ Spend time with a pet.

- ☐ Spend time in nature, or in some other place that's soothing to you.

- ☐ Look for the positives. Often, we get so focused on what happened to cause our sadness that we forget to focus on the positives that may be around us. Look for one good thing that you appreciate each day. After a week, look for two a day. And let this grow.

- ☐ Cry. If you feel like crying, go ahead. It won't last forever—and it's healthier to express what you're feeling than to keep it inside. When you are done crying, ask yourself what you could engage in that would be good for you. Would it be nice to connect with a friend, do some journaling, take a walk? Offer yourself an act of kindness.

Here are some things other kids in recovery have done to cope with sadness.

I take a walk or try to do something in nature when I feel sad.

I tell myself I can't feel good all the time and that I am no longer running from my feelings and that is a good thing.

I now ask myself what I need when I feel sad and then listen to myself. Such as, I need to journal, or I need to call a friend.

DIFFICULT FEELINGS: ANGER

H ere are some thoughts other teens in recovery have had about anger:

I am angry that my parents are always trying to control me.

I am angry that my girlfriend won't trust me in spite of the fact I've been clean for three weeks.

I am angry with myself for getting myself into this situation.

Anger is a natural and normal response to life's irritations, and it plays a role in everyone's life. Anger also exists on a continuum, from being irritated or frustrated to being enraged. When it becomes too intense or lasts a long time, it can be the source of serious problems. Anger can also be directed in different ways. You may be angry with others; you may be angry with yourself.

Sometimes anger is a mask for other feelings (you feel hurt, but you hide it by showing anger). It can also be an expression for attaining control and power (you yell at a person to get them to do what you want). Anger can be retaliatory, finding a way to settle a score. It can be manifested in isolation or depression. For some people, depression is anger turned inward. In some contexts, it is more safe and socially acceptable to be angry than to be depressed.

Anger can also be expressed covertly, rather than overtly; that is, passive-aggressive behavior (expressing anger indirectly), such as procrastinating or being late. Using sarcasm can also be a way of expressing anger. Finally, anger, which is a feeling, can move into rage, which is a behavior. With rage, there is no middle ground. A person who's feeling rage can move from the temperature of 10 degrees to 100 degrees within seconds. Ultimately, anger is its own feeling, and we all experience it.

The following are ways anger is often expressed or handled. *Circle or highlight those you identify with. List any other ways you have expressed anger.*

Yell	Engage in passive-aggressive behavior
Call names	Seek revenge
Punch walls	Isolate
Slam doors	Move into depression
Throw things	Don't ever feel anger
Blame	Other: _____
Be sarcastic	Other: _____

The ways we express anger can sometimes lead to consequences. Describe the consequences you have experienced as a result of the behaviors you circled above.

1. _____

2. _____

3. _____

4. _____

Check the statement that best describes the relationship between your anger and your use of substances.

☐ When I use, it's the only time I can get in touch with my anger.

☐ When I use, it helps numb me. It makes my anger go away.

☐ When I use, I don't have to care about the things that make me angry.

☐ When I use, it's my way of getting revenge at those I am angry at or myself.

☐ I use anger to justify my using.

On a scale of 1 to 10, where 1 is not at all and 10 is definitely, how likely is it that when you use alcohol and drugs, you're using to anesthetize or cope with anger?

1   2   3   4   5   6   7   8   9   10

What have you learned about yourself in this exercise?

_____

_____

What would you gain by handling your anger differently?

_____

_____

The following are suggestions for ways to deescalate the intensity of your anger, communicate in a more constructive manner in order to be heard, and get your needs met.

- When appropriate, assert yourself verbally by communicating with "I" statements, not "you" statements. I statements allow you to say how you are feeling without blaming the other person and putting them on the defensive.

- In conjunction with the I statement, state your feeling, say what occurred that precipitated your anger, and then state what you would prefer in the future should this occur again. Examples of this would be: "I felt angry when you walked away from me when I was talking to you, and in the future, I prefer you would not do that." "I felt angry when you stole my shirt. I would like you to return it and not do that again."

- When you're angry, don't swear.

- When you're speaking to a person you are angry with, sit down. This lessens the energy and makes it more possible to be heard.

- Speak more softly.

Boundaries are particularly important when you're dealing with any emotion, but particularly anger. When you hang onto your anger, it builds resentment, which involves holding on to negative feelings and bitterness about the past. That said, being willing to let go of the anger you feel doesn't mean what someone else did was okay. It means you are willing to walk away rather than pursue the anger. If you let go of the feeling, you are no longer putting your thoughts and energy there. Once you make that move, you may make certain decisions or establish certain boundaries, like resolving to not share so much with that person or to not put your trust in that person in the future. But you don't carry the anger. You make a conscious decision about how you'll behave in the future.

To practice this skill, ask yourself a question when you're angry about something: *Is this matter worth my holding on to?*

If yes, am I justified?

If yes, do I have an effective response?

If not, is there a self-care activity you can do? Below are some examples. Check the ones you think might be helpful for you and add others you'd like to try.

- ☐ Meditate

- ☐ Use distraction—read, call a friend, listen to music, etc.

- ☐ Get physical—exercise, bicycle, play a sport

- ☐ Journal

- ☐ Get creative—paint, draw, play an instrument

- ☐ Other: _____

- ☐ Other: _____

Here are some things other kids in recovery have used to help them no longer feel angry.

I ask myself if I contributed to the situation in any way. If so, I take responsibility for my part.

I go running with my earbuds in.

I ask myself, is it worth my attention? If yes, I pause because I know I have a problem with overreacting. Then I take it to someone who knows me well and we problem solve how I should handle it.

I say the Serenity Prayer, and some days, I say it over and over.

God* grant me the serenity
To accept the things I cannot change;
Courage to change the things I can;
And wisdom to know the difference.

*Many people who use this prayer substitute the word "God" with "higher power" or another spiritual entity of their choosing.

DIFFICULT FEELINGS: GUILT

Guilt is a feeling of regret or remorse about something we have done or not done. It is a feeling we get when we do something wrong—when we've behaved in ways that don't match our values—and we're sorry for our behavior. For example, when we value honesty but lie, we most likely will feel guilt. When we value respecting others but steal something of theirs, we may feel guilt. The good news is that guilt allows us to correct a wrong behavior and get on with our life. That is called making amends.

When you feel guilty but don't take responsibility and make amends, that guilt can eat away at you. You may resort to masking it, and anger is a common mask for guilt. If we're angry at our parents, for instance, we don't have to feel guilty for something we did or didn't do because we've made it so that they are the ones in the wrong. Unfortunately, in situations like this, we often go down the rabbit hole of blaming others. Again, everyone does things for which they feel guilty. When you've been using substances addictively, you are even more likely to do things you will regret.

To be clean and sober and feel the guilt that might arise is tough. But as I said, the good news is you get to take responsibility, and although that takes courage, you have that courage in you. And when you behave with courage, take responsibility for your behavior, and make amends when it's needed, you will like yourself better.

It's important to know that you are not a bad person, even if you have done things you consider bad or hurtful. You're a person like anyone else who sometimes makes mistakes. It's also true that you have probably done hurtful things to yourself, so when it comes to making amends, you may need to make them to yourself as well as to others.

Since you started to use, have you ever...

Lied to family member(s) to hide your use or the consequences of your use?   YES NO

Broken promises to a friend or family member because you wanted to go use?   YES NO

Let go of friends to spend more time with those who were using?   YES NO

Given up interest in activities (sports, arts) that once meant something to you?   YES NO

Rationalized that your drinking or using wasn't problematic (I'm young, I'm just a kid, etc.)?   YES NO

Manipulated a friend or family member for the purpose of going out and getting high?   YES NO

Stolen anything (alcohol, drugs, money, belongings, vehicle, etc.) to be able to use or as a consequence of using?   YES NO

Told someone to get off your back when they questioned your behavior?   YES NO

Witnessed your grades dropping?   YES NO

Skipped class or work to be able to use?   YES NO

Didn't show up to an important event due to using, or showed up to an important event under the influence?   YES NO

Used your sexuality to garner alcohol or other drugs?   YES NO

Called someone names when they tried to confront you regarding your use?   YES NO

Describe the things for which you feel guilty.

_____

_____

_____

When you are using alcohol or drugs, it often gets in the way of your ability to feel guilt, let alone take responsibility for your behavior. Remember that limbic system from chapter 1? That is the drive within the brain that overrides the PFC. The desire to use can override uncomfortable feelings. And guilt feels awful. Take another hit, another drink, another snort, and the guilt goes away. The reward of using can be so strong that you may not feel any guilt. The guilt you do feel quickly gets diminished or nearly evaporates as you rationalize or minimize.

Below are some of the rationalizations we often give that make it easier to just keep using. ***Circle or highlight any you have used and describe other ways you have let yourself off the hook so you don't feel guilty when you are.***

They wouldn't really care.

What they don't know doesn't hurt them.

I deserved it anyway.

They do it, so who are they to talk or judge?

They won't remember.

They deserved it.

Other: _____

Other: _____

When you think, "I want what I want when I want it and to heck with the consequences," it's a setup to engage in something where you cross boundaries, allowing your entitlement to override respect for others. This distorted thinking says: "No guilt means no problem, so no issue."

On a scale of 1 to 10, where 1 is not at all and 10 is definitely, how likely is it you'll use alcohol and drugs to anesthetize or cope with the guilt you might feel in certain situations?

1   2   3   4   5   6   7   8   9   10

Taking responsibility for yourself begins with willingness. Would you be willing to make amends for any of the things you currently feel guilty about?

For the moment, not drinking or using is a start to taking responsibility for your behavior. It's also key that you don't wallow in guilt. The reality is, everyone is guilty of something. You can't get through life without doing something for which you feel regret or remorse. For now, just own the things for which you feel guilty and know that you can and will find ways to take responsibility and come to peace with yourself if you're willing to put in the effort.

There are also ways to cope with the guilt you might be feeling, such as:

- Use affirmations, such as "While I may have done things I regret, I am not a bad person." "Being clean is my first step to making amends." (For more on affirmations and how they can help you as you get and stay sober, see "Exercise: Affirming Self" in chapter 3.)

- Start fresh. Say you are sorry where you can.

- Discuss feelings with others in recovery.

- Get honest about your behavior with someone.

The following are ways kids in recovery have attended to their guilt.

I apologize and work at not repeating the behavior.

I paid back the people I stole from. It took me a while, but I did it, even when they didn't know I had stolen from them.

I try to "do the opposite," with situations I feel guilty about. I felt guilty for causing my brother embarrassment due to my using, and now I spend time with him doing some of the things he likes to do.

I tell myself I am not a bad person, I just did something that was not cool, and I am a better person for addressing it.

OH, YEAH: JOY

While you may have found drinking and using was a way to get rid of uncomfortable feelings, it's also possible that your using was about trying to feel some joy. This exercise will allow you to not only explore that desire to feel to joy but also recognize its presence in your past and ways to experience it in the future. While you may not think about experiencing joy, there are many words on the continuum that you may identify with more, such as "happy," "giddy," "carefree," "satisfied," "pleased," "relaxed," and "peaceful."

If using substances has been your only access to joy for quite a while, it can be helpful to recognize that there may have been aspects of your life previous to your using where you did feel joy. Pause and consider whether prior to your using there were moments or situations in which you felt joy. It could have been with athletics, arts, an accomplishment at school, or time spent with a family member or friend. Know that you can have that feeling again, without being under the influence.

I felt joyful, contented, happy, pleased (any feel-good word) when...

_____

I felt joyful, contented, happy, pleased (any feel-good word) when...

_____

I felt joyful, contented, happy, pleased (any feel-good word) when...

_____

On a scale of 1 to 10, where 1 is not at all and 10 is definitely, how likely is it you used alcohol and drugs to seek out this positive feeling?

1   2   3   4   5   6   7   8   9   10

If at one time using was a way to feel joy, then it's likely that your experience changed when you started to get in trouble with your use. You now find yourself getting high for different reasons. If that is true for you, explain.

_____

_____

_____

Be open to knowing that it's possible to find those positive feelings again. Now that you have been encouraged to look for the positives rather than focus on the negatives in recovery, look for the joy. There are many ways to have that experience.

> **EXAMPLES:**
>
> - Get together with other sober young people and play basketball, go skiing, go to the movies, play board games, or engage in outdoor games.
>
> - Go for walks or hikes with your pet or a friend.
>
> - Practice gratitude.
>
> - Practice "random acts of kindness" or "paying it forward." Simply put, when someone does something kind for you, when the appropriate time shows itself, you offer kindness to someone else. For example, I paid the extra $3.50 someone needed when in line at the grocery store. I also gave up my place in line to a person who was considerably older and physically struggling.

Here are some ways young people in recovery have experienced more joy in their life.

I have had more fun sober, when I genuinely laugh, than I have ever had when I drank.

Since I quit using I truly feel carefree. I feel like I have the whole world in front of me.

The things I have been able to accomplish clean and sober make me really happy.

No more being anxious or agitated, no more scheming...that is joy!

THE GIFT OF FEELINGS

Recovery is knowing what your feelings are and learning how to tolerate them without the need to medicate or engage in other self-defeating behaviors. Still, it can be hard to identify feelings when we have gone to great lengths to avoid them. One of the ways to start to identify them is to notice where they reside in our bodies. Feelings are a felt sense, and recognizing those sensations can help you identify them. Where they are experienced in the body varies from person to person.

Other teens in recovery have shared these ways they identify their feelings in their bodies.

I feel embarrassment in my face, like a hot flush.

I feel sadness in my throat and neck, just stuck there.

I feel anger everywhere throughout my torso, my chest, groin, and into my back.

I feel guilt at the base of my stomach, in my gut.

Focus on one feeling at a time and think about the last time you had that feeling. Go through your entire body and try to identify where you felt that feeling.

Note on the body below where your specific feelings reside when you experience them.

GRIEF

SADNESS

JOY

LONELINESS

FEAR

ANGER

If you struggle with this, the next time you have this feeling, check and ask yourself where you are feeling this in your body. You can also do a quick survey by asking yourself:

- How does my face feel?

- How do my head and neck feel?

- How does my torso feel?

- How do my arms and hands feel?

- How does my belly feel?

- How do my legs and feet feel?

When you listen to your feelings, they will tell you what you need to know. If you aren't scared of them and willing to trust that they are there to help you, to guide you, you will experience the gift. When you first become aware of a feeling, simply observe it and breathe into the feeling.

When you identify and own a feeling, finish the thought with "and I need..."

EXAMPLES:

I feel embarrassed and I need to call my sponsor and talk about it.

I feel sad and I need to just sit with it and allow myself to cry if I feel like it.

I feel angry and I need to take a walk and rethink the situation.

I feel guilty and I need to call my grandfather and apologize for lying to him about the car accident.

Knowing what your needs are gives you a sense of direction as to what to do. FEELINGS lead to NEEDS lead to HEALTHY ACTION. Specific feelings offer many opportunities.

FEAR $\rightarrow$ wisdom, protection, and preservation.

LONELINESS $\rightarrow$ awareness and growth.

SADNESS $\rightarrow$ healing and awareness.

ANGER $\rightarrow$ energy, strength, and assertiveness.

GUILT $\rightarrow$ amends, wisdom, and aligning with values.

JOY $\rightarrow$ connection, excitement, passion, and gratitude.

There are many ways to be present with your feelings. Here are a few suggestions.

- Engage in the arts. They are a great way to express your feelings. Write poetry, write a song, play an instrument, draw, paint, create a collage of pictures, sing.

- Engage in mindfulness practices.

- When you notice a feeling arise, meet it mindfully. "Mindfulness" means open, nonjudgmental awareness of all that arises within—feelings, thoughts, sensations, memories, and more. It can take some work to be mindful of what we're thinking and feeling rather than getting lost in thoughts or feelings or acting impulsively on them. But if you can pause long enough to feel what you're feeling, as nonjudgmentally as you can, or to bring your attention to something like your breath or some aspect of your environment, then you can begin to establish a different relationship with your own feelings.

- Think about someone you care about—a younger sibling is a good choice—and ask yourself, "If they were in my situation, what would they be feeling?" It is often easier to be empathetic toward another person rather than yourself. Putting them in your situation is a step toward realizing the feeling you are hiding.

- Put a feelings list in a strategic place around your house, such as your bathroom mirror or refrigerator, in your car, or on your phone. Develop a ritual of looking at the list three times each day and asking yourself, "What do I feel?" "Okay" or "nothing" is not an answer; we're always feeling something. If you still can't identify what you're feeling in a given moment, ask yourself where you experience it in your body and what that body part is telling you.

- Create feeling boxes. You can do one big box or a box for each of the six feelings identified in this book. When you are taking stock of your day, write down the feelings you've had on different strips of paper and put them in the box. Write a brief note about the situation that triggered the feeling. Once a week, go through your box and take out the feelings you have found a way to cope with. Think about the remaining ones, and if you aren't sure what you can do, reach out to someone you trust and talk about it.

- Create a feelings journal where you track and write about how you feel on a given day.

- Talk to your feeling. Journaling is a great way to have a conversation. You might start with a hello. Tell it you are aware it is there and exists. You can write about the circumstances that are creating the feeling. Tell it anything you want. Conclude with thanking it for speaking to you.

- Reach out to a support person—someone you trust and can talk to.

Here are some ways other kids in recovery have become comfortable with their many feelings.

I just get really honest with myself and allow myself to have the feeling. I don't necessarily act on it. I just feel it.

I tell myself to keep breathing and know that this will pass.

I ask my feeling what it needs.

I observe it, noticing where it is in my body. If I want to let it go, I visualize it becoming splintered into bits and watch it disintegrate.

MOVING FORWARD

Knowing your feelings is a big step in your recovery. If you use the tools you now have available, you'll be able to stay present with them, listen to them, and be open to their guiding you to recognize what you need. You will find freedom in no longer denying them, hiding them, or drowning them in substances.

This grounding meditative practice, and the others throughout the workbook, is an additional tool for when you find yourself feeling anxious, restless, or uneasy. Visit http://www.newharbinger.com/53356 for an additional exercise on feelings, "Matching Insides with Outsides."

GROUNDING: CIRCLE OF LIGHT

1. Sit comfortably in a chair or lie down with a pillow under your head and another under your knees. Place one hand on your chest and another on your belly.

2. Take a very slow, deep breath. As you count to yourself, about two numbers per second, draw air down toward your belly. Breathe deeply enough for both the hand on your belly and the hand on your chest to move. Count up to six as you inhale.

3. Let the breath out naturally.

4. Breathe in again very slowly, counting to six, feeling both hands rise. Release the breath and let it flow out. Continue this breathing until you feel safe and relaxed.

5. If it feels safe, gently close your eyes; otherwise, just lower your gaze.

6. With your next inhalation, imagine a large circle of healing light forming in front of you. This circle of light can be whatever size, shape, or color your imagination wants it to be.

7. When this circle of light is fully formed, picture yourself stepping into it and letting it slowly surround you.

8. With your next inhalation, breathe in as much of that healing light as you wish. Do this for several breaths.

9. Then with each exhalation, let go of any tension in your body and any worries, distress, or troubling thoughts in your mind.

10. For a few minutes, continue to breathe in the healing light and breathe out the tensions, worries, and distress.

11. When you are ready, gently open your eyes or lift your gaze.

CHAPTER 3

LOOKING FOR THE POSITIVE

LIVING WHAT YOU VALUE

Every day we make choices—some small, others significant. Each may influence our future in major ways. Most often, choices are determined by our system of values. Values are beliefs about what's most important to us. They are demonstrated by the way we choose to act. Values are invisible to others; what people see are our behaviors.

Here are values some kids in recovery say are important to them.

Having lots of friends is one of the most important things to me.

Looking good is important.

I think it's important to be kind to animals and the elderly.

Being good in the arts is important to me.

Review the following list and circle the values you feel are important to you and fill in others not mentioned here.

Responsibility	Accomplishing goals	Honesty
Friendships	Independence	Fitting in
Intelligence	Closeness with family	Money
Being respectful	Environmental concerns	Compassion
Being funny	Being artistic	Life
Other: _____	Other: _____	Other: _____

Some of the behaviors that brought you to this workbook may have come from losing touch with your values since you began using substances.

Put an X across any of the values above that you once had but have gone by the wayside.

Next, pick a few of these values and describe times you lost touch with them when under the influence of substances.

EXAMPLES:

VALUE: Responsibility

Knowing I was going out to use, I lied about where I was going. I didn't do my school work as I wanted to go party. While I say I value responsibility, I don't show it very much anymore.

VALUE: Honesty

I was stealing money from my mom, my brother, and my friends to get drugs. If they confronted me, I acted like I was the victim.

1. VALUE: _____

_____

_____

_____

2. VALUE: _____

_____

_____

_____

3. VALUE: _____

_____

_____

_____

4. VALUE: _____

_____

_____

_____

Sometimes your values get you in trouble. Consider this story from a teen in recovery.

I used to value being funny. When I was using, I thought I was funny because people laughed at me. I got attention and I liked that. But being funny meant doing stupid things, like stealing from people. I really wasn't funny and the people laughing at me were loaded and just making fun of me. Being funny should not involve hurting other people. My being funny violated values like honesty and consideration of other people. I think being honest and considering others might be better values for me.

Have you had any values that got you in trouble or ended up having a negative effect? *If yes, describe how.*

_____

_____

_____

Getting in trouble with alcohol and drugs doesn't mean you're a bad person. It means you did things that violated your value system, and in doing so, you hurt yourself or others. The good news is you can choose to act from a place of healthier values.

Consider some of the values that feel like ones you really want to live by now. Which behaviors would help you live each value?

Example:

VALUE: Responsibility

BEHAVIOR THAT SUPPORTS THIS VALUE: I'll show up to work on time and not leave early.

1. VALUE: _____

BEHAVIOR THAT SUPPORTS THIS VALUE: _____

_____

_____

2. VALUE: _____

BEHAVIOR THAT SUPPORTS THIS VALUE: _____

_____

_____

3. VALUE: _____

BEHAVIOR THAT SUPPORTS THIS VALUE: _____

_____

_____

Most of us don't take time to think about what we value until we find ourselves not liking ourselves. Knowing what your values are is a good map for future decisions about how you live and a way back to feeling good about yourself and what you do.

STRENGTHENING THE VALUE OF HONESTY

There are many values that will support you in your recovery process, but there are a few that are foundational, and honesty is one of them. Honesty can lessen guilt, demonstrate self-respect, and show responsibility.

On a scale of 1 to 5, where 1 is not at all and 5 is all the time, rate how honest you have been about your behavior and its impact on you and others.

1   2   3   4   5

Would the person who knows you the best agree with the rating you gave yourself?   **YES NO**

Now, write a letter to yourself.

1. Start with the salutation, such as "Dear (first name)."

2. Begin by telling yourself you haven't been so honest while using and give some examples.

3. Then tell yourself how you will benefit if you become more honest with yourself and others.

4. Conclude the letter by showing yourself some compassion.

Here is an example from another teen in recovery.

Dear Anthony,

You have been doing a lot of lying to other people for a few years now. Sometimes you outright lie and tell your parents you are in school when you dropped out three months ago. You tell your girlfriend you are busy studying and can't see her when, really, you are out using with your buddies. Then you tell yourself what others don't know doesn't hurt them and that your smoking weed doesn't really hurt you when you are getting more paranoid by the day.

You need to admit to yourself you have been lying, or not telling the truth, by minimizing situations or making excuses. If you got more honest, you could put your life back together; you wouldn't have to hide out from the people you love. If you got more honest, you could face your problems head-on. You are not a bad guy. You can do this.

Anthony

Dear _____,

STRENGTHENING THE VALUE OF RESPECT

Another value that will support you in your recovery process is respect for others and yourself. Respect for others is shown by behaviors that demonstrate that you value them, such as:

- Showing up when you are supposed to

- Following through with what you say you will do

- Having healthy communication and not blaming or criticizing others

Respect for yourself is shown by behaviors that demonstrate that you care for yourself, such as:

- Wearing clean clothes at the start of each day

- Taking care of financial responsibilities

- Exercising and eating healthy foods

On a scale of 1 to 5, where 1 is not at all and 5 is all the time, rate how respectful you have been toward others and then yourself.

Respectful of others

1   2   3   4   5

Respectful of yourself

1   2   3   4   5

Would the person who knows you the best agree with the ratings you gave yourself?   YES   NO

What are three ways you can show more respect to others?

1. _____

2. _____

3. _____

What are three ways you can show more respect to yourself?

1. _____

2. _____

3. _____

STRENGTHENING THE VALUE OF CARING

Caring for others and for yourself is important to your recovery process, but people often lose sight of this when they are under the influence.

On a scale of 1 to 5, where 1 is not at all and 5 is all the time, rate how caring you have been toward others and then yourself.

Caring toward others

1 2 3 4 5

Caring toward yourself

1 2 3 4 5

Would the person who knows you the best agree with the ratings you gave yourself? **YES NO**

What are three ways you can show caring toward others?

1.
2.
3.

What are three ways you show caring now, or could show caring, toward yourself?

1.
2.
3.

COUNTERING RISKY THINKING

When we are reactive and engage in risky thinking—thinking that sabotages our ability to see situations accurately and can lead to self-defeating behaviors—we can quickly get ourselves into trouble. There are several ways we put ourselves at risk for distorting and making situations more difficult. And every one of us does it at some time or another.

The following are common ways our thinking can undermine us. *Circle or highlight the descriptions you know you engage in.*

Overgeneralize

You take the experience of a moment and cast it over all future possibilities.

Thought: My girlfriend just dumped me and now no girl will ever want to be with me.

Mind Read

You make assumptions and conclusions without knowing the facts.

Thought: I can tell by the way he looks at me that he doesn't like me.

Catastrophize

You always see the worst-case scenario.

Thought: I know I won't pass this class and then no way will I get into college.

Reject the Positive

You don't allow yourself to experience something positive by insisting it doesn't count.

Thought: She was really nice to me, but I know she didn't mean it.

Overestimate

You overestimate the odds of a negative outcome.

Thought: If I call my brother and ask him for a ride home, I know he'll say no.

Blame

You don't take responsibility for your behaviors and blame others for your actions.

Thought: I wouldn't have yelled at you if you hadn't yelled first.

Shoulds

You impose a set of expectations that aren't based in reality, are unrealistic, and include judgment.

Thought: I'm old enough that I should be able to know how to do that.

Name the thinking styles you engage in and describe two situations in which you engaged in it, and what happened. (If you need more space, you can use another sheet of paper.)

THINKING STYLE: _____

    1. _____

    _____

    2. _____

    _____

THINKING STYLE: _____

    1. _____

    _____

    2. _____

    _____

Now, consider how you could take responsibility for your risky thinking in the future. Here are some examples from other teens in recovery.

I used to blame everyone for all my actions that got me in trouble. But the truth is no one makes me do anything. I am responsible for myself.

I don't see every problem now as a catastrophe. I label it a problem to be tackled and I think about what I can do, or how I'll get through it.

I let go of telling myself and others they "should" by not being judgmental and being more compassionate or understanding of the circumstances.

Here are some ways to counter risky thinking.

- Be willing to look for the positive in a situation.

- Stay away from words that are absolute, such as "never," "always," "everyone," and "no one."

- Stay away from words that are strong indicators you are engaged in distorted thinking, such as "stupid," "false," "hopeless," "pointless," or "unfair."

- When you're complimented, pause, count to ten slowly (which allows you to not focus on discounting it), and say, "Thank you."

- Stay away from finger-pointing or starting sentences with "you." Instead, use "I" statements to articulate how you feel.

- When you hear yourself thinking or saying "should," stop. Take a breath. Then tell yourself there is no "should." Focus on what is, as clearly as you can.

- Don't make assumptions; ask for more information.

- Use the affirmation "I'm responsible for my own behavior."

GETTING TO KNOW YOUR INNER CRITIC

P icture yourself busy with a project, and as you work on it, you have music playing in the background. Day after day working on your project, the music plays, over and over. You aren't even paying attention to it because you're focused on your project, but at some point, you realize you've been unconsciously singing along or tapping your foot the whole while.

Like the music in the background, we all have a part of our thinking that can be called our Inner Critic. The Inner Critic loves to tell us what is wrong with us: "You're just so stupid." "No one really likes you." "You'll never amount to anything." You may have become so accustomed to the messages from your Inner Critic that you no longer hear yourself using them, but there they are, chipping away at your self-esteem and self-confidence.

Draw a picture of your Inner Critic and surround it with its favorite words. What's it saying to you?

Think about your Inner Critic's favorite haunts. *Does it show up when you're at home or school? Does it show up at work or when you are with friends? Does it show up when you weigh yourself or when you look in the mirror? Write those places here.*

_____

_____

_____

_____

We all have an Inner Critic. It can also cause us a lot of problems when we listen to it. Your Inner Critic probably:

- Stops you from taking healthy risks.

- Stops you from setting healthy boundaries for yourself.

- Undermines your courage to change.

- Views your life as a series of mistakes waiting to happen.

- Makes you the victim to the judgment of other people.

- Is so terrified of being shamed that it monitors all your behaviors to avoid this.

- Doesn't allow you to take in the good feelings that other people have toward you.

- Prevents you from chasing your dreams.

When you become skilled at demeaning yourself, you don't even hear it. So, thinking about the music in the background, imagine turning the volume up loud. Start paying attention to what you're saying to yourself. When you recognize yourself caught up in self-defeating thoughts, you can stop it. You have the choice to turn down the volume, switch songs to something kinder and more compassionate, or turn it off completely. Here's how.

1. Recognize what you're telling yourself.

2. STOP and ask yourself: Where did this come from? Whose voice am I hearing?

   Asking those questions helps you recognize that this is something learned and it's not a part of who you are. No one is born disliking themselves; it comes from messages we received—from family members, people at school, or other instances when someone was critical.

   When your inner voice is being critical, it often conveys its message as though it were definitive. If it says, "You're stupid," the implication is that it is not to be refuted. The tone of your Inner Critic is often one of disgust. If it says, "You can't ever get anything right," the implied message, via the tone, is that indeed you never will get anything right.

3. Counter the message. Get out of the all-or-nothing thinking and give yourself an example of it not being true. So, when you say, "I'm just a loser," counter that with "I'm not a loser; I recently helped this friend out who was really hurting." Or when you say, "I'm really stupid," counter that with "I'm not stupid; I've made some good decisions for myself." Then remind yourself of your new message.

   You can also have fun with your Inner Critic, like giving it a silly name. Some people have called their Inner Critic names like Faker, Blamer, Ms. Danger, Judge, or Mr. Negativity. When you hear it rearing its ugly head, call it by its name and tell it to quiet down. Tell it you're not going to pay attention. You are not listening; you're changing the music!

AFFIRMING SELF

Affirmations are positive self-talk, phrases or statements used to challenge negative or unhelpful thoughts: "I am creative." "I have something to offer people." "I can succeed in recovery." They have the power to motivate you to act on your values, concentrate on achieving your goals, and change negative thinking patterns and replace them with positive thinking. They help you access a new belief system and counter negative messages that may be controlling your life.

Affirmations fire up certain neural pathways and change areas of the brain that make you happy and feel positive. They help you create the reality you want. When you self-affirm regularly, you become more likely to dismiss harmful messages, from both your Inner Critic and the world around you, and respond instead with the intention to change for the better. And you feel a strength you didn't previously feel. You feel more confident. You feel more self-assured.

Yet, most people start their affirmations with hesitation. I hear young people say,

That's ridiculous.

That's crazy.

No way that works.

Yeah, sure. There's no way thinking or telling myself I have value will actually make me feel it.

If this suggestion seems strange, know that others your age who tried it really came to like it.

Oh yeah, I thought it was stupid, but what did I have to lose? I was told to try doing them twice a day for a week. So, I did. And at first it felt weird, and I thought it was going to be a total waste. But after five days, I realized I felt better and I felt empowered. Something was shifting. I kept it up and now it's a regular part of my day. I do them each morning and night, and sometimes in between when I feel I need to remind myself of my strengths or worth.

For affirmations to work and make lasting long-term changes in the ways you think and feel, you do need to practice using them regularly. It's best to work with your affirmations daily for at least ninety days so it becomes a habit that you find ease in doing and totally enjoy. A helpful way to start the affirmation process is to make a declaration statement of a positive change you want to make. A declarative statement could start with:

"I am learning…"

"I am willing to…"

"I am discovering…"

"I am becoming…"

EXAMPLES:

"I am learning to say no."

"I am willing to set limits."

"I am discovering I am courageous."

"I am becoming confident and secure."

Be concrete. Use the present tense ("I am"), keep it short and simple, and avoid negative phrasing. For instance, rather than saying, "I am no longer afraid to be assertive," say, "I am assertive."

More definitive affirmations would be:

"I am a unique and capable person just as I am."

"I am deserving of good things in my life."

"I take responsibility for me."

"I am setting limits for myself."

Write your affirmations down here. Shoot for between three to five affirmations to start.

Once you have your affirmations, begin working with them three times a day. Choose a setting and time during which you are most relaxed, not apt to be interrupted. Prior to saying your affirmations, take some deep breaths. Then say your affirmations slowly, with feeling and a sense of conviction. Repeat a second time, just as slowly. Repeat a third, fourth, and fifth time. While it may seem silly or awkward, try to trust the process.

Repeating your affirmations, and saying them with feeling, are two primary methods for reinforcing them—and any new pattern of thinking. Writing down affirmations and having them accessible to read when you need them will also be helpful in reminding you of your strengths. You might carry them on a card in your pocket, purse, or wallet, or keep them on your phone, computer, bathroom mirror, refrigerator, etc.

Here's one last affirmation for you: I deserve recovery. Yes, you do!

LOOKING INTO THE FUTURE

Living your values, letting go of risky thinking, changing your thinking, silencing your Inner Critic, affirming yourself—all the recovery skills you are working on in this chapter set you up for exciting life possibilities.

Imagine yourself a year from now having lived with your new skills and in recovery. Write yourself a letter about your accomplishments. Here's an example from a teen in recovery.

Dear Kaylee,

You finished your junior year in school and are going into your senior year. You made the soccer team. You connected with a few of your previous friends you missed. Your little sister is now looking at you as a role model and wanting to spend time with you. Your parents are trusting you again, giving you more freedom. I am happy for you.

Kaylee

Dear _____ ,

_____

_____

_____

_____

_____

You have a lot you can look forward to and have begun the process. Feel good about the work you're doing.

MOVING FORWARD

Remember, recovery is a process, and it doesn't take place overnight. It's easy to get tempted to revert to old ways, so stay close to your support people and be kind to yourself. Don't put unrealistic expectations on yourself and don't assume you'll feel great about everything. You are choosing to live life in a way that you will feel good about yourself. Visit http://www.newharbinger.com/53356 for additional exercises on affirmations ("Affirmations") and shifting negative thinking ("Changing Perceptions and Feelings").

Here is a brief grounding exercise that can be helpful during times of stress or when you simply want to boost your mood or reinforce staying grounded.

GROUNDING: HEALING COLORS

1. Sit comfortably on a cushion or on the edge of a chair with your back straight but not stiff.

2. Breathe slowly and deeply for a minute or two. Close your eyes and take a few more deep breaths.

3. Imagine a place of beauty and safety. This might be the bank of a river or a sandy beach; it could be on the deck of a boat in calm water or your favorite place in nature. It is your place to imagine, but it implies safety and beauty.

4. Now envision yourself in that place. If you are outdoors, imagine a breeze on your face; if you are indoors, imagine a gorgeous view out a nearby window.

5. If you like, you can be alone in this place. Or if you prefer, one or more people with whom you feel safe can be there with you.

6. As you continue to breathe deeply, imagine that colors are starting to appear around you. Don't try to create any particular colors; let them emerge naturally. These are colors of love, of nurturing, of safety. They may be blues and purples, oranges and reds, or yellows and greens. Whatever colors help you feel safe and relaxed, let them arise and fill the space around you. Continue to take gentle breaths.

7. Stay in this place of safety and beauty for as long as you like. When you are ready, open your eyes and resume your day. Know that you can come back to this place anytime you choose.

CHAPTER 4

NO LONGER HIDING

THINGS HAPPENED

What do you think of when you see the word "trauma"? People often think of trauma as a big event, such as a car accident, being in a natural disaster, or being caught in a community shooting. Those events can certainly be traumatic, but there are also other traumas—for instance, losing someone significant due to death. You may have lost a parent, a sibling, a good friend, or someone else close to you due to illness, an overdose, a suicide, or an accident. Nor is death the only kind of loss that can be traumatic. Perhaps you were very close to a friend or family member and they moved away. Bullying and cyberbullying can also be very traumatic, particularly at this time in your life when you are developing your sense of worth and identity. To be perceived in any way as different from others, to be overweight, underweight, to not be wearing the cool clothes, to be physically challenged, or to be part of the LGBTQ+ community puts people more at risk for bullying and ostracization.

Growing up as a person of color in Western societies subjects you to racism and the consequences of racism. For some, racism has been a phenomenon that their family has had to contend with for multiple generations.

Physical and sexual abuse are much more common than you probably know, for both males and females. Physical abuse includes being hit, but it is also being slapped, pinched, or slammed. And to witness that happening to someone else is also traumatic because your sense of helplessness is overwhelming. Sexual abuse and assault, whether by a family member or someone you may or may not know outside of the family, may have been a precursor to abusing alcohol and drugs. As well, the likelihood of being sexually assaulted substantially increases when you are under the influence of alcohol and drugs or engaged in a drug transaction.

When the event behind the trauma is obvious and acute, such as those mentioned, they are often referred to as "big T traumas." You are even more likely to have what is described as "little t traumas," experiences that are traumatic to your well-being that are more subtle and ongoing. Whether the experience is a big T or little t, it results in the belief that you don't have value, there is something wrong with you, or you are not good enough. This can be a significant factor in your desire to drink and use. In no way, though, is the term "big T" meant to diminish the impact of those examples referred to as "little t." What is traumatic for you, big T or little t, is significant.

Below you'll find lists of big T and little t traumas. Some of the events on the little t list may not become traumatic if they occur only once or a few times, but they create traumatic stress when they are cumulative and repeated. Circle any of the traumas you may have experienced. This exercise, and what you've read in this section, may provoke intense feelings. Be sure to take the time you need to complete it.

LITTLE T TRAUMAS INCLUDE:

Unrealistic expectations by a parent

Failing at something important to you

High stress at work or school

Harsh, unfair, or extreme criticism

Rejection by a parent

Being compared unfavorably to
another family member

Being yelled at, ignored, disrespected,
or discounted

Loss of a long-sought-after goal

Being controlled by someone you trust

Discovering the infidelity of one parent
to another

BIG T TRAUMAS INCLUDE:

Bullying

Sexual assault

Serious car accident

Public shooting

Being the victim of a crime

Experiencing acts of racism

Living with community violence

Witnessing others being abused

Experiencing the death of someone
close to you

Mental health problems in family

Growing up with chronic neglect

Physical abuse in family

Addiction in family

Incest

Note if there are other traumatic situations you have experienced that are not listed.

_____

_____

What are you thinking right now?

_____

_____

_____

What are you feeling right now?

_____

_____

_____

If you are feeling vulnerable and need a brief break, that's understandable. You may find it helpful to turn on some comforting music, have a nourishing bite to eat or drink, take a brief walk or run, do some deep breathing, or reach out to a support person.

Sometimes seeing all this on paper makes trauma more real, particularly when we have tried to cope with it the only way we know how—for instance, with substances. Experiencing any kind of trauma is difficult at best for anyone, but when you are young, it's even more confusing and more hurtful. You may find yourself asking why this has happened to you or whether you'll ever feel or be "normal."

If you have a history of trauma, drugs and alcohol can quickly become a solution to the pain and shame of that trauma. Trauma has a strong connection to people's desire to use. ***Circle any of the items below that describe your relationship between the trauma you have experienced and your use of alcohol and drugs.***

Alcohol and other drugs are good medicators; they anesthetize emotional pain.

Under the influence, you might feel a sense of power, strength, or confidence that you don't normally feel. In the moment, it feels good—perhaps so good that you don't plan to give it up.

Alcohol and other drugs may loosen you up and enable you to at least temporarily forget your pain and troubles.

Perhaps, when you use, you feel free.

Here are some thoughts from other teens about trauma and their desire to use.

Bullying started in grade school and kept up; using and dealing was my way to get on top of it.

My parents divorced when I was eight, and my dad moved across the country. I changed schools four more times in the next few years, and my mom wasn't home a lot. I just got lost in the world of drinking and drugs.

Whatever has happened to you that has been traumatic, you did not deserve it. There are people who can help you work through the impact it is having on you. When you experience things that are traumatic, it is common to not tell anyone. You already feel alone, and trauma reinforces that aloneness.

Who in your life could you share this information with?

It's important to know that what you have experienced does not define you. You didn't deserve to be subject to behaviors that made you believe you are not worthy, not lovable. You can heal from your trauma, but to do so, it is necessary to stop using substances because they will interfere with the healing process.

Here are some ways teens in recovery have healed through traumatic events.

I had never talked about my mom's death, ever... I never talked about the flashbacks I had, ever... I just drank and used into oblivion. Thank heaven I got sober, and it gave me a chance to come to terms with what happened.

I thought only girls were sexually assaulted, but in recovery I have found that it has happened to guys too. And I don't have to use to cope with it anymore. I have written music, written poetry, it all helps.

My family looked so perfect, I thought we were, but now I realize that it was loaded with little t's. No wonder I hated myself and always felt different. Cannabis was my solution to all of that. Understanding trauma has helped me not let the shame I felt about myself run my life.

Thinking about trauma you have experienced can create vulnerability, so don't hesitate to engage in some self-care, such as a good walk or run, listen to nurturing music, having a nourishing snack, or doing some deep breathing.

FREEDOM FROM THE PAIN OF GRIEF

It's likely as a teen or young adult you already know someone who died in an accident or from an illness, an overdose, or perhaps even by suicide. Maybe you've lost more than one person. Perhaps you were very close to these people; other times, not so close. Nonetheless, they were a part of your world. It's also possible these deaths occurred within your family, either expected or sudden and unexpected. Either way, it's painful.

There are other losses that cause pain, such as when a best friend moves away, or you move and need to change schools. Maybe you've lost a romantic relationship. Or maybe you have a parent who has become preoccupied with other aspects of their life and doesn't show up for you as much as you need them. That too is a kind of loss.

The pain of loss and grief is part of the human condition. We learn and grow from it. Hopefully, we do so with support and love. But depending on life circumstances, we may be walking this journey alone. Many of us don't have a safety net at these vulnerable times; we don't have support or people there to guide us and help us cope. Substances often become the crutch to coping. We don't know what to do, so we do what we know.

While it is very common to want to run from pain, this just pushes the pain down the road, creating more pain for us. The following exercise will offer you some insight, direction, and skill in processing the grief you have experienced. *Circle or highlight any of the losses you identify with.*

- Death of family member

- Death of pet

- Death of friend

- Loss of an important opportunity (school, goals, work)

- Change of schools

- Absent parent

- Loss of romantic relationship

- Loss of significant material things

- Moving from friends or family

- Other: _____

Naming your losses on paper is a way of acknowledging them. *Try putting the events you circled on a timeline. See one teen's example below as a guide.*

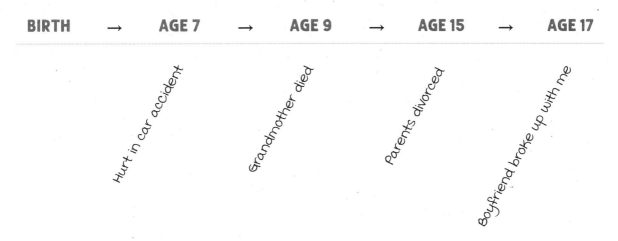

BIRTH → **AGE 7** → **AGE 9** → **AGE 15** → **AGE 17**

Hurt in car accident

Grandmother died

Parents divorced

Boyfriend broke up with me

Now, create your own timeline, note your current age at the far right, and then insert approximate ages at which you experienced a significant loss.

BIRTH → → → → **TODAY'S AGE**

Naming your losses can be emotionally powerful. Take a moment to ground yourself with a deep breath before you move on. If you want to take a break, you are welcome to do that also, but make a commitment to yourself to come back to this.

Reflect on your timeline and take a moment to explore the various ways your grief has affected your life.

How has grief affected you emotionally? (For example, are you finding yourself moody, sad, angry, agitated, etc.?)

_____

_____

_____

How has grief affected you socially? (For example, do you find yourself isolating, or only wanting to hang around your family, acting aloof when with friends, etc.?)

_____

_____

_____

How has grief affected you physically? (For example, are you sleeping more or less, eating more or less, engaging in self-harm, etc.?)

_____

_____

_____

How has grief affected you mentally? (For example, are you ruminating on the loss, finding yourself spacing out, etc.?)

_____

_____

_____

How has grief affected you spiritually? (For example, are you questioning the meaning of life, angry with your God or a higher power, etc.?)

_____

_____

_____

Is there any possibility that your grief has had an impact on your drinking or using? If so, describe.

_____

_____

_____

This is a very personal journey and we all do it differently. But it is not one to take alone. You deserve to find comfort in this process, and to have your process honored.

There are many ways to express your grief. The following are some things other young people have done to help them heal from their grief.

I played the guitar at my friend's gravesite.

I attended Al-Anon to cope with my dad's absence.

I go running and allow myself to scream.

I ran a marathon in my brother's name.

Here are some other common ways people express their grief or console themselves.

- Music

- Photography

- Writing

- Creating a memory book

- Talking to a friend or family member

- Planting a tree or flowers in a special place

- Connecting with mutual friends

Do you have healthy ways to be with and express your grief? If yes, describe them.

There is no specific timetable for moving through a grief process. With some losses, there will always be pain. In time, the intensity of it will lessen if we allow ourselves some healthy outlets for what we feel. *Name a few additional ways you are willing to address your loss.*

Finally, know that in your grief you have the right to all of your feelings. Everyone experiences grief in their own unique way and you don't have to tough it out. You can tell people what is and is not helpful. My hope is you can claim your own meaning from what has happened and find ways to honor your losses.

LIBERATING YOURSELF FROM SECRETS

Are there any secrets you keep deep inside? We often think that if our secrets were known, we would be judged as bad, less than, or not as good as others. Yet, holding in feelings associated with secrets can lead to suffering. And it's not just the content of the secret that can hurt us, but also what we do to keep it hidden. It's very likely your using is a way to numb the pain or just obliterate the secret from your mind. But it's right there again the moment you're not under the influence.

When we haven't shared something that we feel bad about it takes on greater power, and often that power becomes bigger than it ever needed to be. If you stop using or drinking and are in a recovery process, but are still keeping secrets, the pain is often the reason for starting to drink or use again.

How can you tell whether you are living with a secret? One way is to ask yourself: "Am I hiding something from someone?" and "Is there something I feel I can't tell anyone because I'm afraid of what might happen?" If so, remember, that's just an assumption. If you widen your options of safe people, you'll find there is someone trustworthy and accepting of what you share.

When we carry secrets:

- Our view of the world becomes distorted.

- We are in a defensive position with others because we are always on the alert to protect our privacy.

- We may become very closed and protective, which gets in the way of being genuinely close with others.

Here's the truth: Whatever you did or whatever you experienced is not a statement about your worth or value. You are not your secret.

In this exercise, you won't be asked to write down your secrets. Simply reflect on whether you're keeping any. They are often secrets about things that are going on in your family, or about behaviors you have engaged in, or things that happened to you. Sometimes it is all those things.

Now, try thinking a little differently. Think of your secret becoming a confidence you share with safe people, those whom you feel are trustworthy. It may feel scary, but finding a safe person to share your secret with can deflate the secret's power. *List some possible safe people in your life. It could be a certain family member, a friend, a partner, a counselor, a physician, or a person in your recovery group.*

_____

_____

_____

Remind yourself of some of the reasons to share secrets rather than keeping them inside.

- It relieves a burden. You no longer have to continue to lie to others.

- It allows you to be true to yourself.

- It prevents a possible surprise discovery.

- It enables you to have a more honest relationship with another person.

- It makes it possible to make amends.

- It makes it possible to begin the healing process.

Do you think it would be helpful for you to share a secret(s)?   **YES NO**

Are you ready?   **YES NO**

You can take this in small steps. You don't have to begin with sharing several secrets; just begin with one that feels safest. You can also begin by being open about your feelings: "I have a secret I would like to share, but it's hard for me to do that" or "I have something I would like to share that I haven't talked about before." From there, you could say why you want to share: "I think I will feel better about myself if I do" or "The pain of keeping secrets is driving my use of drugs." And if you need something from the person you are sharing with before you disclose the information, tell them what that is. For example, you could say, "I need to know you will not laugh," "I need to know you will listen to my full story," or "I need you to not tell anyone else at this time."

If it's a therapist or physician you choose to share your secret with, they will inform you of the circumstances in which they cannot keep what you share confidential. You can then decide whether or not to disclose to them.

Whenever the conversation happens, and however it might go, be compassionate with yourself. You are working on you, and that is huge. Take this step when you are ready, and you'll figure out what needs to happen on the way. Remind yourself of the gifts that can come with sharing more about yourself and that you're worth it.

The following are gifts some young people found as they let go of painful secrets.

Once I started to be honest about what I kept hidden, life got so much better for me.

I did not deserve what happened to me! And it does not have to be my secret.

I was so tired of carrying the guilt I had, so when I finally was able to talk about it, while embarrassed, I felt nothing but relief.

LETTING GO OF SHAME

❝ Stupid." "Broken." "Bad." "Less than." "Damaged." "Defective." "Not good enough." "Worthless." These are all words we use when experiencing toxic shame, the belief that we don't have value. We don't think, "I feel shame." Instead, we think, "I'm not good enough" or "I'm damaged." This type of inner dialogue erodes our self-confidence and self-esteem and can only hurt us.

When you experience this unhealthy form of shame, you feel defeated and alienated. You feel as if you don't deserve to hang out with your friend, that you are on the outside looking in at your family. You may even feel as if you don't belong to the human race. When you feel a lack of worth, there is also a sense that your vulnerability is exposed. This can make you go to great lengths to hide from others or project a false image. But you're not born thinking or behaving this way. It's something you learn, often from outside sources like your family or larger culture.

The messages you've internalized may have been verbal, such as:

- You're so stupid.

- Why can't you just be like your brother/sister/the other kids at school? (This implies you need to be different than you are to be okay.)

- You are just like your mom/older brother/cousin (someone you know who's generally not liked and considered "bad").

- You are never going to amount to anything.

- Other people are more important than you.

- You are not worthy of anything.

Shame-based messages can also be the result of experiences. When someone is angry, disappointed, or upset with something you did or said, they may, instead of speaking to you about your behavior, attack your worth and value. *Did you hear messages that made you feel inadequate or not good enough? If so, describe.*

Shaming messages also come from aspects of society, such as music, videos, blogs, podcasts, or possibly even the faith you have been introduced to. *Have you heard messages that imply there is something wrong with you? If so, describe.*

Experiencing intolerance of race, sexual orientation or gender, or physical differences can also fuel the belief that you're not okay, something is wrong with you, and you need to be different. *Are there any shaming messages you internalized about your ethnicity, race, gender, sexual orientation, or physical abilities? If so, describe.*

Using substances is often a way of medicating your shame-based beliefs. Substances can give you a false sense of bravado or provide a connection to others when that is difficult. But using doesn't make the shame go away; it just becomes hidden.

You deserve to know your value and to be able to connect with others without needing to prove yourself. You are worthy just as you are. It's not your fault that these messages were imparted to you, but it is now your responsibility when you recognize you are acting them out. Otherwise, there's no way that your self-talk and the possibilities for your life will change. You can't change the past, or other people's past or present behavior, but you can change what you do with these messages and choose to no longer act them out.

Recognizing Yourself in Toxic Shame

What are the signs you're feeling toxic shame? For some, it's when we tell ourselves things like "I'm stupid" and "I can't get anything right," or when we feel utterly alone and think things like, No one likes me. Or we act it out when we isolate or self-harm.

Write down some of the signs you're feeling toxic shame.

_____

_____

_____

Shame-based messages are often imparted as though they're nonnegotiable. For example, "I'm so stupid. I can't ever get anything right." Now counter it with a thought that gets you out of the all-or-nothing thinking: "I'm not stupid; I just didn't take time to think it through. I know how to do lots of things well" or "The other day I helped my little sister with a problem she was having in her history class." Shame-based self-talk often includes the words "never," "always," and "should," so be alert to them. Shaming statements are frequently said with disgust, so listen to the tone in which you speak.

The following are affirmations for you to consider.

"I don't deserve to hurt myself."

"I'm smarter than I think."

"I have worth."

"I deserve better."

What can you tell yourself?

When you're using these affirmations to counter shame-based messages, say them from a place of compassion for yourself. Think of how you'd behave with someone you care about, such as a sibling or a little kid in the neighborhood. Extend that same kindness to yourself.

You may also feel shame because of your own behavior. When using substances, it's easy to do things for which you feel ashamed. While toxic shame is more of a self-punishing belief, being ashamed is often reflective of healthy shame—shame that serves to acknowledge "I did something bad" and guides you toward self-correction, making amends, and growth. You learn from the experience of healthy shame and move on. Toxic shame, on the other hand, is harmful psychologically because it is self-punishing and lingers on. Here are the nuances of shame:

TOXIC SHAME = I am bad

ASHAMED = A feeling state associated with healthy shame

HEALTHY SHAME = Seeing the behavior as bad, but separating it from your worth

If you conclude you are a bad person for your "bad" behaviors, then you have bypassed healthy shame and there is no opportunity to learn from the situation. You have turned to shaming yourself, fueling more toxic shame. It's critical to let go of distorted thinking and say no to toxic shame messages. Any "bad" behaviors you engaged in don't make you bad. You may be a person who made bad choices, and possibly behaved horribly, but that doesn't mean you lack value; it means you acted outside of your values. Otherwise, you would not be feeling ashamed.

Finally, it's not unusual to feel shame about things that have happened to you while under the influence. You may have been subject to a sexual encounter or assault that was shaming. Or, possibly, you may have been drugged unknowingly when you were out partying, and that led to being more out of control, or made it easier to do something you realized later was irrational or wrong, such as doing something illegal.

Whatever happened to you, or whatever you did, may have been horrific, and hurtful to you or to another, and it's probably very painful to acknowledge. But it doesn't make you an unworthy person. And there are ways to make amends to yourself and others.

Here are some mantras you can use as you continue to work through shame:

- "I did things I am ashamed of, but that doesn't mean I'm a bad person."

- "Bad things that happened to me don't make me bad, defective, or unworthy."

- "I have value and worth."

WHERE DO I FIT?

As a young person, this is a time when you're moving toward greater connection with friends and peers, challenging your dependency on parents or caregivers, navigating changes in relationships with siblings, and finding your path as an independent person. Changes in the family are natural, but they often become problematic when you're getting into trouble with drugs and alcohol.

How has your family responded to your using? Some members may be angry; others guilty, scared, confused, or embarrassed. They may have sought guidance for how to help you, or not. They may have made amends for wrongs they've done, or not. In the end, you have the choice of recognizing how your behavior contributes to your family's health. When there is poor communication, lying, and manipulating, you contribute to its impairment. When you listen with respect, are honest, and make amends, you contribute to the family's health. These teens captured the conflict that was happening in their families:

> I've not been thinking about anyone in my family. I just was out for a good time and it was all about what I wanted right now.

> I feel guilty about all the fighting I caused at home.

When you think of your family, list three adjectives you would use to describe your family unit prior to your using—for instance, "confusing," "hostile," "safe," "loving," "scattered," or "disconnected." (If you grew up in more than one family, do this exercise for each family you lived with and note the number of years you were with each different family.)

1. _____

2. _____

3. _____

If that has changed since you began your use of alcohol and drugs, use three adjectives to describe this shift and describe it.

_____

_____

_____

Now that you have looked at the family system, this is an opportunity to look at the different relationships within your family. List your primary family members (e.g., parents, stepparents, siblings, grandparents), and then next to each, describe how you felt about them prior to your using and then after you began using.

EXAMPLES:

1. Name: mom	Prior to using: caring, loving	After using: distant, sad
2. Name: Dad	Prior to using: distant	After using: angry
3. Name: Brother	Prior to using: fun, connected	After using: distant

1. Name:	Prior to using:	After using:
2. Name:	Prior to using:	After using:
3. Name:	Prior to using:	After using:
4. Name:	Prior to using:	After using:

What did you discover?

_____

_____

_____

While you may want your family to change their ways, you only have the power to affect your own behavior. Your relationship may be so distant or unhealthy due to a family member's personal struggles that any changes you make would still be limiting in getting your needs met. Nonetheless, consider ways you could be more accountable for your part of the relationship that honors what you value. It is also possible you may decide that keeping distance, or having rigid boundaries about how much time you spend with them or what you are willing to share, is what is best for your recovery.

Would you like to make changes to any of those relationships?   **YES NO**

Consider what you can do. You might also journal about this situation or speak up in a recovery group to get feedback.

_____

_____

_____

You may want to have an honest conversation with certain family members. The point of these conversations is to make your thoughts and feelings known and to be accountable for yourself. It is not to convince, elicit forgiveness, or manipulate. You can begin to take responsibility for your part in the relationship, and set the stage for a different future, by using the following sentence stems.

- "I have assumed you know, but in case you do not, I would like to tell you..."

- "My use of drugs and alcohol has affected our relationship in these ways..."

- "Traits I value in you are..."

- "I feel close to you when..."

- "In order to improve our relationship, I'm willing to..."

Here's how other teens in recovery have used these sentence stems.

I have assumed you know, but in case you don't, I would like to tell you I wasn't just drinking; I was using pills too.

My use of drugs and alcohol has affected our relationship in these ways: I lied to you. I used you.

I feel close to you when we play video games together, or walk the dogs, and when we find things to laugh about.

In order to improve our relationship, I'm willing to call you more often, to not use alcohol or drugs, and to follow through with my commitments.

Pick a family member that you feel safest with and write out what an honest conversation could look like. Then repeat this exercise with the other family members you named. When done, consider which ones you might be willing to share with. Decide whether you want to share in a conversation or a letter. If you are working with a therapist, take their guidance as to good timing for this. Sometimes family members are not in a space to listen, so if you choose to share, know your intentions and let go of expectations. If you feel unsafe, not ready, or this wouldn't be helpful to you at this time, consider writing a letter and hold on to it for possibly sharing at a later time. Visit http://www.newharbinger.com/53356 for an exercise, "Listening: The Other Side of Communication" for tips on how to structure a respectful conversation.

I was so afraid my dad would always hate me for what I did, but once I got more honest with him, our relationship really began to change.

I scared my little brother so much in my using that they avoided me. Now that I am clean, they love being around me and we have a good time together.

My relationship with my mother will probably never be perfect. It may not ever fully heal. But I feel better about my ability to communicate with her and to behave toward her in the ways I value.

MOVING FORWARD

By addressing the exercises in this chapter, you're taking your recovery seriously, and that's more than commendable: it's courageous. This is the time to remind yourself of what you learned in chapter 2 regarding feelings. Use the tools suggested to be able to stay present with whatever feelings you are having. Practice self-care, and share with others. This is all a part of putting the pain of the past behind you as you move forward. Visit http://www.newharbinger.com/53356 for an additional exercise, "Acknowledging the Unspoken."

While the following grounding activity can be practiced at any time, it's especially helpful when you need to let go of a painful memory, thought, image, or feeling.

GROUNDING: PALMS UP, PALMS DOWN

1. Sit comfortably, with your back straight, but not stiff. Close your eyes or lower your gaze. Bring your attention to your breathing.

2. Take a slow, deep breath. As you do, count to four slowly—one, two three, four—at a rate of about two numbers per second.

3. Then exhale, counting slowly to four once again.

4. Repeat steps 2 and 3 four or five more times, until your breathing is slow and relaxed.

5. As you continue to breathe slowly and evenly, hold your hands out in front of you with your palms facing up. Leave your elbows at your sides or stretch out your arms fully, whatever feels more comfortable.

6. Take as long as you need and imagine your hands holding all the difficult thoughts, feelings, and events that you've experienced. Feel their weight.

7. When ready, turn your palms over so they're facing down. Imagine all the troubling energy you've been carrying dropping to the ground. After a moment, shake out your hands.

8. Turn your empty palms back up. They are now ready to receive positive energy, supportive thoughts, good feelings, and help from others. Hold your palms in this position for ten to twenty seconds.

9. Slowly open your eyes or raise your gaze.

CHAPTER 5

STAYING THE COURSE

KNOWING YOUR TRIGGERS

Triggers are specific memories, situations, and behaviors that have the potential to jeopardize your recovery. Some triggers are unique to the individual; others are more common. One common trigger is euphoric recall. Euphoric recall is romanticizing using experiences and forgetting about the negative consequences. When you talk about your using and drinking, do you focus predominantly on the good or exciting times? If your answer is yes, that is euphoric recall.

For example, you talk about how fun the party was, but neglect to mention that afterward you had an accident and wrecked your parents' car. If you and others are sharing mutual storytelling, these "war stories" become even more powerful and contagious. Sharing such stories is a way of bonding, but it's critical you catch yourself in these dialogues and refocus on where that previous behavior took you. You can bond with new experiences that don't sabotage your life.

If you continue to engage in euphoric recall, it's easy to think how nice it might be to have "just one more good time." Sadly, with addiction, once you go "back out," your life often quickly disintegrates into more negative consequences and fewer good times.

Another common trigger is friends and family who still use. You may have already realized that to experience recovery, you'll need to let go of many of your drinking and using friends. Outside of using together, you likely have little reason to stay connected. But this can be difficult because you might have some fun memories. Even when certain relationships aren't the best for us, ending them can be hard.

You may be thinking, "I can still have these friends. I just have to not use with them." Unfortunately, going to the same places, seeing the same people, and telling yourself you can handle it is a big threat to your recovery. This is the time to take stock and reconnect with friends you left behind to be with using friends. Be open to new friends who can identify with you being clean and sober. Recovery can give you fantastic friendships.

To prevent pressure from your using friends, you may choose to let them know you are in recovery and you won't be in contact. It's helpful to delete these friends (and any dealers) from your phone and social media sites. Many young people in recovery ask a friend or other support person to help them do this. The support makes it easier and helps you be accountable.

Not spending time with family members who are triggers is not always an option. In that situation, you will have to plan ahead how to handle the relationship in the future. It most likely means having clear boundaries for yourself about what you will and will not do with them, where you will go, and how much time you spend with them. Setting boundaries for yourself and with others, particularly with family, will require a lot of support. Seek guidance from other recovering friends or talk to a therapist for support.

Both friends and certain family members can exert pressure. Remember how the brain works: the sights, smells, and sounds associated with the people you used with can make your limbic system light up. Add euphoric recall as a factor, and all the willpower in the world can dissolve.

In addition, social situations can be significant triggers. Family events such as reunions, weddings, and funerals or work or school events may be places where you regularly used. There may be certain friends' homes that were easy to use and drink at, or hangout places where you frequently used.

Again, think about self-care strategies you can use in risky social situations. Some examples:

Choose not to attend.

Limit your time.

Tell specific people who can offer you support while there that you're in recovery before you go. Let them know ways they can make this a safe environment for you.

Plan what you're willing to participate in before you go. For example, if this is a family reunion, you might stay away from specific areas where people are drinking or smoking. And you might plan to participate in games or other activities to keep yourself occupied.

Provide your own transportation so you're free to leave when it best suits you.

If you're engaged in a 12-step program, talk to your sponsor prior to the event or situation or take another recovering friend with you.

Talk to others in recovery about the successful strategies they've used in similar situations.

When you think about your slippery slope, what can you foresee to be your triggers? Be specific. (For example, it may be your current girlfriend, your older brother, the upcoming high school graduation, or a family vacation.)

1. **TRIGGER:** _____

2. **TRIGGER:** _____

3. **TRIGGER:** _____

4. **TRIGGER:** _____

Identify the options you have regarding the trigger or how to best take care of yourself in the situation.

1. **TRIGGER OPTIONS:**

_____

_____

2. **TRIGGER OPTIONS:**

_____

_____

3. **TRIGGER OPTIONS:**

_____

_____

4. TRIGGER OPTIONS:

_____

_____

These are serious considerations. It's important to be proactive in eliminating certain triggers or knowing what you will do to lessen the impact of a trigger. But you can do this. You've already taken many significant steps in this recovery process.

RECOGNIZING OVERCONFIDENCE

Overconfidence—a sense that you have the answers and there is no value in hearing input from others—is a major threat to recovery. Signs of overconfidence include:

- Being unable to hear what others are saying. Even if you've initially listened to what others were saying when you began this recovery process, often, as you feel better about yourself, there's a huge risk in no longer hearing what others have to say that has value to you. You might find yourself thinking, "I know what's best for me. I got the message, I'm back in control now. You don't know me."

- Rejecting ideas without trying them out. You may be asked to do things in recovery that are scary or confusing or that you have certain preconceived impressions about. For example, you decide you won't like someone before you meet them, or you attend a self-help meeting and within the first ten minutes decide it has nothing to offer you. It's easy to sabotage your recovery by thinking, "That's not what I need."

- Wanting immediate results. There's a tendency in recovery to be unrealistic in your expectations and want immediate results. For example, you might think, "I haven't used or drank for eight weeks and my parents still don't trust me enough to let me live on my own." The thinking here is, "I expect that because I've been in recovery, the world should give me what I want and give it to me now. If it doesn't, then why should I put all this effort into my abstinence?" This is an attitude of expecting others to reward you because you've given up your use of alcohol and drugs. That's dangerous thinking. Ultimately, you're attaching more value to your experiences under the influence than what you're gaining in your recovery.

Rate how much you identify with each specific sign of overconfidence on a scale of 1 to 10, where 1 means you identify with it very little and 10 means you identify with it completely. If you rate yourself 2 or higher, describe two examples and the outcome.

BEING UNABLE TO HEAR WHAT OTHERS ARE SAYING

1   2   3   4   5   6   7   8   9   10

EXAMPLES

1. _____

2. _____

OUTCOMES

1. _____

2. _____

REJECTING IDEAS WITHOUT TRYING THEM OUT

1   2   3   4   5   6   7   8   9   10

EXAMPLES

1. _____

2. _____

OUTCOMES

1. _____

2. _____

WANTING IMMEDIATE RESULTS

1   2   3   4   5   6   7   8   9   10

EXAMPLES

1. _____

2. _____

OUTCOMES

1. _____

2. _____

Are you willing to address these issues? If yes, with whom and when will you discuss them?

_____

_____

The next time you find yourself in one of these patterns of overconfidence, it may be helpful to reach out to someone with more recovery time than you and ask for feedback. Challenging your self-talk is important, such as reminding yourself that recovery often means doing life differently from how you have done it before.

What might you do to compensate for signs of overconfidence?

_____

_____

Confidence is a fine attribute, and you may have things to feel confident about, such as excelling in music, the arts, sports, or connecting with people. Yet, when it comes to recovery, there needs to be a respectful fear of the power of substances and how quickly you can get back into thinking patterns that are ultimately self-defeating.

MOVING BEYOND RESENTMENTS

Resentment is a common emotional reaction to the experience of feeling discounted, slighted, wronged, or unheard. There's a 12-step saying that says holding on to resentments is the equivalent of swallowing poison and hoping the person whom you are resentful toward will die. A Buddhist perspective describes anger as an acid that eats away at the vessel holding it.

Resentments are often built on assumptions: "She's not looking at me; she is disrespecting me." They are also built on entitlement, a form of unrealistic expectations combined with impatience: "Now that I'm in recovery, my girlfriend should trust me." Thinking that begins with "I'm owed…" or "I deserve…" often reflects a resentment.

The following are examples of resentments that people have as they explore recovery.

> I resent that in recovery it isn't wise for me to attend certain school events.

> I resent my parents not giving me the money I want.

Many people say they are resentful about anything and everything when they first come into recovery. They resent that the sky is blue or ice cream is cold. When you are resentful, you see the world through a skewed and dark lens. This happens when you're scared, insecure, and don't feel empowered.

Are you carrying any resentments? If so, identify a few of them.

1. _____

2. _____

3. _____

How do you think hanging on to these resentments affects you?

While many resentments are based on assumptions, unrealistic expectations, and impatience, sometimes they are built on the fact that you have been wronged. *Does that influence the resentments you're feeling? How so?*

If yes, is it possible you have a part in creating the situation in which you feel this resentment? (For example, you may be resentful the judge isn't dismissing your driving violation. Your part would be that you were the one arrested for driving when you were under the influence.) If you are hanging on to resentments, see if you can identify your part in creating the situation.

Ultimately, who is paying the price for hanging on to resentments?

Are you willing to let go of your resentments?　　　　　　　　　　　**YES　NO**

If not, what do you get from holding on to them?

_____

_____

_____

_____

One of the ways to move away from resentment is to ask, "What is my resentment potentially covering up?" It often covers up fear, guilt, feelings of inadequacy, pride, or self-doubt.

Do you think your resentments are covering up anything for you?　　　**YES　NO**

To move away from a place of resentment try the following:

- Identify what the resentment is covering up.

- Ask yourself what your part is in the situation you resent.

- When assuming, check it out.

- Put yourself in someone else's shoes, which may allow expectations to be more realistic.

- Be willing to live and let live.

Keep in mind that when you hold on to resentments, your focus is directed externally. As long as your attention is directed toward others and what they have or haven't done to you, it's difficult to pay attention to what you can do to engage in behaviors that support your recovery.

A helpful antidote to resentments is the regular practice of affirmations and gratitude. Practice the affirmation: "I can choose between living in resentment or with acceptance. I choose acceptance."

HONORING YOURSELF IN RELATIONSHIPS

Young people often give away too much of themselves with others. This is a serious trigger for using behaviors. If you haven't internalized your own self-worth, or don't feel a very strong sense of yourself, you can easily be dependent on the acceptance of your friends or romantic partners to feel worth and value.

What is critical about this in recovery is the tendency to put more importance on friendships and romantic relationships than recovery practices. But you don't want to lose sight of your needs and wants and forget your priorities.

The following are indicators that you are losing yourself while in friendships or relationships. *Check any that you identify with.*

☐ You tend to ignore or minimize your feelings.

☐ You do things you don't want to do to make the other person happy.

☐ You tend to apologize or take the blame to keep the peace and avoid conflict.

☐ You have an excessive need for approval from others.

☐ You'll do almost anything to avoid feeling rejection.

☐ Your wants and needs consistently take a back seat to others' wants and needs.

☐ You are constantly thinking about the other person.

☐ You experience guilt or anxiety when doing something for yourself.

☐ You take on more work than you can handle to lighten someone else's load.

Identify two people with whom you've experienced those indicators, either now or in the past. Describe the experience.

1. **NAME:** _____

   What happened?

   _____

   _____

   _____

   _____

2. **NAME:** _____

   What happened?

   _____

   _____

   _____

   _____

If you forsake your own well-being for another's—acquiescing to another, attaching your worth to another, putting most of your energy into supporting another—then you may be acting in a codependent manner. Codependency is an unhealthy dependence on a relationship and a drive to seek outside validation or approval to feel value and worth.

A big clue you are in or pursuing an unhealthy relationship is when you are hiding it from others.

If current relationships of yours reflect codependent dynamics, here are helpful steps to reinforce healthier relationships.

- Be honest about the relationship with another person you trust and listen to their feedback.

- Be willing to meet people halfway, but expect them to do their part.

- Read books about codependency to educate yourself about it.

- Create a daily journal listing times you engaged in codependent behavior. Identify what you could do differently in that situation should it happen again.

- Write a list of what you lose when you engage in this behavior and what you gain if you do not.

- Practice daily affirmations and remind yourself that your needs and feelings are as important as anyone else's.

It can take time and disciplined effort to break free of codependency and pursue relationships in which you matter as much as the other person. Young people in recovery describe the benefits this brings.

I find myself being with people that I don't spend all this energy trying to please, and focus on just having fun.

I don't walk around anxious all the time.

I don't waste my energy trying to fix something or someone that I didn't break.

I feel better about me.

FINDING YOUR RECOVERY COMMUNITY

This workbook is meant to help you find new ways to cope and change your outlook from fear and negativity to one of hope as you engage in recovery. Being able to continue this means finding a strong support system in which to enjoy life, have friends, have good times, and be there for each other as you navigate daily joys and struggles. Finding support groups of other young people who are substance-free is vital to your recovery. They will remind you, when needed, of where your using took you and the gifts of sobriety and being clean. Ultimately, recovery is about connection with yourself and with others.

Types of Groups

There are many possibilities for finding support. Some groups are specifically for young people. There are also groups that honor ethnic and cultural differences and gender-specific groups. While the social connections are what young people find most inviting, these groups also have a structure that allows you to maintain the values of recovery, such as:

Honesty	Hope	Courage	Integrity	Willingness
Humility	Love	Justice	Perseverance	Service

Many of the most prominent self-help groups for substance use have emanated from the 12-step group Alcoholics Anonymous (AA). It's truly impossible to name all the groups, but popular ones are Narcotics Anonymous (NA), Cocaine Anonymous (CA), and Marijuana Anonymous (MA).

AA and related groups do have a strong spiritual basis, in that you're encouraged to recognize a higher power—but this higher power can be anything you choose, from God to nature to the group itself. They also welcome the atheist and agnostic. Also, they don't ask you to claim you're addicted. The only requirement is a desire to stop drinking or using.

There are also religiously affiliated groups, including Millati Islami World Services, which supports Islamic recovery chapters; JACS (Jewish Alcoholics, Chemically Dependent Persons, and Significant Others), which guides individuals through recovery in a nurturing Jewish environment; and Celebrate Recovery, which offers a Christ-centered 12-step program.

An alternative to 12-step programs is SMART Recovery (Self-Management and Recovery Training). It's a community of peer support groups with no religious or spiritual basis that help people recover from addiction.

For support regarding childhood trauma and being raised in a dysfunctional family, there is ACA, originally for adult children of addiction, but open to others from different types of challenging families. There are also Alateen and Al-Anon groups to help you cope with others in your family system who are addicted to substances.

There are college recovery programs. Several colleges have sober living dorms and areas for sober study and connecting with others. Many states have social organizations that provide recreation and service projects for young people, such as YPR, Young People in Recovery. These programs can be readily located on the internet.

There are clearly many options here. You don't have to know right away which program is best for you. Just don't reject the idea without trying it out.

Working with a Group

Self-help groups are not cults; no one's there to brainwash you. They are programs of attraction, meaning you get to find out what they can offer you and you have choices about whether or not to engage. But there is some advice you can follow. Wherever you choose to go, go more than once. And go to different ones. Look for what you like, not what you don't like. Look for the similarities between you and others, not the differences. Remember, you don't have to know whether or not you are addicted; you just need to know that you'd like to not use or drink. You aren't expected to share if you don't want to.

These programs often have steps that will help guide you in recovery, and they offer fellowship, which is about finding others in recovery to share time with. Most groups also have an opportunity for you to find an individual support person who is considered a sponsor or mentor.

Sponsors are not therapists, but they can offer direction and guidance. Finally, wherever you are in the world, some form of group support will be available to you, at no financial cost. Visit http://www.newharbinger.com/53356 for helpful resources.

Other young people who reached out for group support have found it helpful.

I went to groups that were known for having young people, but came to learn that many of the older people had a lot to offer me too.

Going back to school was scary, but I quickly got associated with other sober kids in the school's recovery support program and we have a great time together. Now I'm completing my four-year degree and know the career path I want.

Wherever I go, for whatever reason, there's always a recovery meeting I can go to.

Identify three advantages for meeting others who are on a similar recovery path.

1. _____

2. _____

3. _____

If joining a recovery group is something you're interested in, work with adults and others you trust to find a group and try it out.

LIVING IN GRATITUDE

Gratitude is about focusing on what's good in our lives and being thankful for the things we have. It's pausing to notice and appreciate what we often take for granted, taking a moment to reflect on how fortunate we are when something good happens, whether big or small.

Gratitude is a wonderful antidote to fear- and anger-based emotions. It's like a U-turn on complaining or thinking about what we don't have. The more you engage in active gratitude for what is good in your life, however small, the more quickly you move away from resentment, depression, and anxiety. Gratitude can open you to more positive emotions, like happiness, calm, joy, and love. You can build better relationships when you feel gratitude and express it to others in your life. And it allows you to celebrate the present—and staying in the present is critical in recovery.

There are many words to describe gratitude, such as "thankful," "lucky," "fortunate," "humbled," and "blessed." Do you identify with any of these words? How might you change the way you perceive things to tap into gratitude?

As you practice recovery skills, gratitude may come naturally. But for most people, it takes practice to develop. You might build a habit of paying attention to things you're glad you have in your life. Slow down every so often and notice what's around you. Ask yourself, "What's good about this moment?"

You might also work to share your appreciation more often. Try using these sentence stems:

"It really helped me out when..."

"You did me a favor when..."

"Thank you for listening when..."

"I really appreciate it when..."

"I am grateful for..."

You might also engage in kindness to inspire gratitude in others, such as opening a door for a stranger or giving back through volunteering.

Finally, try keeping a gratitude journal. Each day, write down three things for which you are grateful, be it people, places, objects, moments, or successes. This is a simple yet profound exercise to build into a daily ritual to increase your ability to be and feel grateful.

You can start your practice right now. ***Try identifying three things you're grateful for today. You can be grateful the sky is blue, or the sun is shining, but if you can, make the gratitude a bit more meaningful.***

Today I'm grateful for _____ .

Today I'm grateful for _____ .

Today I'm grateful for _____ .

MOVING FORWARD

It is an incredible journey of self-discovery and honesty to go from recognizing where you may be vulnerable in recovery, to finding a support system to sustain recovery, to recognizing the gifts of recovery. It's not always easy, but hopefully you're beginning to see the gifts of recovery, such as self-respect. You deserve to feel good about yourself and the depth of work you are engaged in. Visit http://www.newharbinger.com/53356 for an additional tool, "Packing for a Spiritual Journey," to further explore self-discovery.

Anytime you feel anxious or distracted as you continue your recovery journey, use the following exercise to help you stay centered and focused.

GROUNDING: YOUR FIVE SENSES

1. Sit comfortably. Close your eyes or lower your gaze. Take a few slow, deep breaths in and out until you feel relaxed.

2. When ready, open your eyes or raise your gaze and silently, one by one, identify five different things you see around you.

3. Close your eyes or lower your gaze and identify four things you hear.

4. Continue to breathe slowly and identify three touch sensations.

5. Now identify two things you smell.

6. Finally, identify one thing you taste.

7. Continue to relax, and when you are ready, open your eyes or raise your gaze.

CHAPTER 6

CLAIMING RECOVERY

FUN IN RECOVERY

When young people consider recovery, one of the first questions they ask is, "How will I ever have fun again if I'm not using?" In such moments, recognize that asking that very question implies you may be in euphoric recall (see "Exercise: Knowing Your Triggers" in chapter 5). It's very likely that by now those good times have been replaced with shame, guilt, fear, and problems related to school, work, money, and legal issues.

Recovery is an invitation to try new things that many young people find fun, exciting, even meaningful, without having to be under the influence. *Circle or highlight those you have an interest in and list additional ideas you have.*

- Rock climbing, mountain climbing, hiking

- Painting, drawing, writing, learning another language

- Snowboarding, skateboarding, waterskiing, snow skiing

- Going to the gym, taking dance classes, taking acting classes

- Playing pickleball, volleyball, tennis, soccer

- Horseback riding, motorcycle riding, bicycle riding

- Sewing, knitting, craft making, woodworking

- Going to concerts, playing an instrument, writing music

- Traveling, camping, swimming, cooking, baking

- Hanging out with friends

- Other: _____

- Other: _____

Who are some people in your life you might be able to do these things with?

_____

_____

Excitement also comes in other forms, such as the enthusiasm of being accepted to a particular program at school or work, accomplishing a goal such as a half-marathon, or performing in a school play. *What life events or achievements do you foresee that could be exciting?*

_____

_____

Here's what other young people in recovery have to say.

I skied the black run this past winter and never could have done that when I was using.

I was accepted into the design program I had always fantasized about and my submission was done clean and sober.

When my non-using friends and I go out, we act crazy singing and dancing without being under the influence. We aren't sick later, we don't do things we regret, and we remember the good time we had the next day.

CHOOSING ABSTINENCE OR RECOVERY

As you are nearing the close of *Your Recovery, Your Life*, this is a good time to seriously evaluate whether you are in genuine recovery or in an abstinence-only mode. In other words, is your commitment to life without substances more about avoidance (avoiding substances, avoiding people, and avoiding taking responsibility for decisions and behaviors) than it is about recovery (refraining from distorted and addictive thinking, being honest with yourself and others, being accountable for your behavior, and genuinely embracing life without substances)? Being honest about the degree you are practicing recovery or abstinence in the various areas of your life can offer you direction as to where you want to heighten your focus.

Take a moment to review the different areas of life below. For each area, circle A for abstinence (avoidance) or R for recovery to indicate whether you believe you're demonstrating abstinence or recovery behavior. If you circled R, how is your recovery being experienced or demonstrated in this area of life? If you circled A, what would be helpful for you to do to shift from A to R?

EMOTIONAL HEALTH   A   R

_____

_____

PHYSICAL HEALTH   A   R

_____

_____

FAMILY RELATIONSHIPS   A   R

_____

_____

FRIEND RELATIONSHIPS

A R

_____

_____

SCHOOL/WORK

A R

_____

_____

It's not always easy to assess your own behavior. If you're struggling to assess yourself in any of these categories, or if you're struggling to figure out how you can shift from abstinence-only mode to recovery mode, try talking to another person in recovery you trust. **_Describe the situation or behavior you are struggling with and identify who you may be able to reach out to._**

_____

_____

_____

_____

It can't be said enough that recovery is a process and you need to applaud yourself for the recovery you're experiencing. You can and are doing this. There may have been times when you were your own worst enemy. Now, you have the choice to be your own greatest champion.

KNOW THE WARNING SIGNS

Imagine a flight crew preparing a plane for takeoff. They perform a rigorous examination of the plane and go through an extensive list to ensure the safety of the plane and everyone on the flight. Should anything problematic be found, they have specific procedures to address the situation.

Recovery is much the same. If you know the warning signs, you can monitor whether or not any addictive behaviors, patterns, or signs of relapse are occurring. And if you have a specific plan to address the warning signs, you can put that plan into action anytime you might need to. This worksheet is also available at http://www.newharbinger.com/53356, if you need to assess your risk of relapse in the future.

Below are some common warning signs of relapse. *For each sign, rate where you would place yourself now, with 1 being not at all and 10 being all the time.*

I have no interest in my appearance.	1	2	3	4	5	6	7	8	9	10
I'm discouraged about the future.	1	2	3	4	5	6	7	8	9	10
I rarely participate in recovery meetings.	1	2	3	4	5	6	7	8	9	10
I'm distant from family and friends.	1	2	3	4	5	6	7	8	9	10
I don't enjoy activities.	1	2	3	4	5	6	7	8	9	10
I don't like to listen to others.	1	2	3	4	5	6	7	8	9	10
I feel resentful.	1	2	3	4	5	6	7	8	9	10
I have secrets.	1	2	3	4	5	6	7	8	9	10
I feel ashamed.	1	2	3	4	5	6	7	8	9	10
I feel depressed.	1	2	3	4	5	6	7	8	9	10
I think I could control my using.	1	2	3	4	5	6	7	8	9	10
I think I could use and not get into trouble.	1	2	3	4	5	6	7	8	9	10
I don't care if I get into trouble.	1	2	3	4	5	6	7	8	9	10
I'm hanging out with using/drinking friends.	1	2	3	4	5	6	7	8	9	10
I'm spending hours online.	1	2	3	4	5	6	7	8	9	10
I'm missing work or skipping classes at school.	1	2	3	4	5	6	7	8	9	10

Ultimately, all these signs need to be taken seriously. *But with any signs that you rated 7 or above, identify steps you can immediately take to strengthen your recovery.*

1. _____

2. _____

3. _____

List names and phone numbers of three people you can call should you experience difficulty with any of these warning signs.

1. _____

2. _____

3. _____

Put this information in places you can readily access it, such as on your phone, on your bathroom mirror, on your laptop, or inside your wallet or purse.

Here are some strategies that other teens in recovery use when they feel their recovery is tentative.

I engage in more recovery meetings.

In recovery meetings, I listen more and talk less.

I share more in recovery meetings and am open to feedback.

I call another recovery person, and keep calling until someone answers.

I use a 12-step sponsor or therapist more often.

I make a nightly plan for what I will do the next day that supports my recovery.

I get out of bed the moment I wake up and look at my recovery plan.

I make sure there is food in the house.

I ask for help.

KEEPING PRIORITIES IN PERSPECTIVE

In order to maintain recovery, it's helpful to see how your day reflects your priorities.

Divide the circle below into pieces representing your priorities. Consider time spent at school or work, time spent with friends or family, recreation, and time devoted to recovery practices or being with recovery friends. How big a slice of the average day's "pie" does each of these areas take up? For example, if your job and family are of equal importance, each would have equal space in the circle.

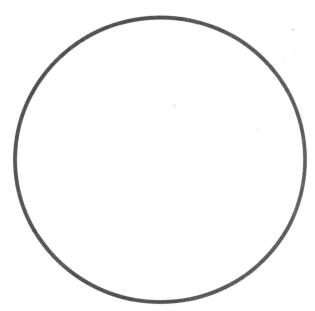

Now that you have divided the circle based on your priorities, which piece or pieces are the largest?

_____

Which piece or pieces are the smallest?

_____

How large a piece is your recovery practice?

Are you satisfied with the percentage of the circle you gave your recovery practices? Yes / No

If recovery activity is one of your smaller percentages, your recovery is in serious jeopardy. If that is true, in time, the other areas that are important will suffer. Consider what would happen to those larger pieces you prioritized should you relapse.

You are more likely to reach your goal of ongoing recovery if you know how much time you want to put into the specifics of recovery practice. *If the following circle were to represent your recovery practices and activities, how would it be divided? Consider time spent attending 12-step/recovery meetings, reading recovery-related materials, listening to recovery-related podcasts, being engaged in mindful practices, talking with a sponsor, or socializing with others in recovery. Include any other recovery practices you are engaging in.*

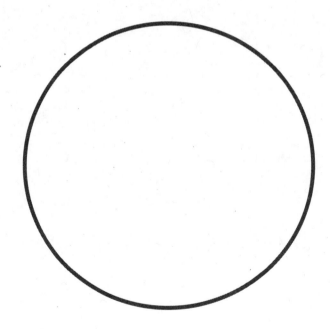

The following is what other teens have said that has helped them to maintain their priorities.

I do a weekly check-in with my sponsor in my NA program.

Each morning, I start my day with a gratitude check.

I write in my journal every night, noting what recovery practice was helpful for me that day.

I talk to myself and remind myself I like myself a lot better these days due to being clean and sober.

PRACTICING DAILY REFLECTIONS

An important part of recovery is taking time each day to reflect on how that day has been for you. It gives you the opportunity to pause and consider your gratitude practice and guide you to make healthy decisions. Some people do this at various times throughout the day; others tend to do this regularly at the close of the day. Some reflect independently; others do it in groups or with other recovering people.

Daily reflections require sitting with yourself and taking an honest moment to think about what has transpired. What worked? What didn't work? What could be done differently? Without reflection, it's too easy to forget these things. Reflection also offers the opportunity to practice intentional focus.

Take some time to come up with your daily reflection routine. What kind of setting do you think would best support this practice (for example, journaling in your bedroom, being with another person)?

What time of day do you think would work best for you?

The following is an outline of a daily reflection exercise. Try this today. This exercise is also available online at http://www.newharbinger.com/53356, so you can print out as many copies as you need.

Validate yourself for the little steps you took today that demonstrate recovery. Often, we think recovery is taken in leaps and bounds, but it's the little steps along the way that keep you in the recovery zone. Allow yourself to realize the good things you are doing (for example, "I overheard ex-friends planning their night out partying. In the past, I would have... But today, I...").

What did you do today that supported your recovery?

If you found constructive ways to combat self-defeating thoughts, feelings, or behaviors, what were they?

Were you resentful today? If so, what actions do you need to take?

Were you dishonest about anything today (with another or yourself)? If so, what actions do you need to take?

Did you do or say something today out of fear? What was it?

Is there anything you did today for which you need to make an apology?

Have you kept something to yourself that should be discussed with another person? If so, what was it?

_____

_____

If you have additional reflections that support your recovery, add them to your daily reflections.

_____

_____

Close with an affirmation, a gratitude statement, or a favorite prayer.

If you practice daily reflections routinely for a couple of weeks, it will become more natural. These reflections help keep the focus on recovery.

MOVING FORWARD

In recovery, you can have great friendships and a wonderful, exciting life. You will be better able to identify your goals and achieve them. You can keep your priorities intact. You have the ability to know your warning signs of not being engaged in recovery behaviors, reach out for help, and listen to the feedback of others. It's not overwhelming when you stay focused on today. One day at a time, you can do this. Visit http://www.newharbinger.com/53356 for an additional tool, "Those Pressing Questions," that young people often have in early recovery.

The following grounding visualization is a great way to honor your priorities, feel more at peace, and embrace this recovery process. Use it and the many other grounding exercises repeatedly to help you embrace your recovery, and your life.

GROUNDING: EXPERIENCING RECOVERY

1. Sit in a quiet, comfortable place, uncross your arms and legs, and close your eyes or lower your gaze. Slowly take several deep breaths.

2. As you breathe in, visualize a warm, healing energy coming into your body. As you breathe out, imagine stress and tension slowly leaving your body. Take three deep breaths in…and out.

3. Say to yourself, "Today I let go of my expectations. I let go of my fears." Visualize any expectations and fears flowing from your body, and your body and spirit being surrounded by healing energy. Allow yourself to feel the safety of that energy.

4. Scan through your body and become aware of where you may be holding any resentments. Feel that place and slowly breathe healing energy into it. Continue to breathe and slowly say to yourself, "Today I release my resentments. They no longer serve me." Visualize those resentment floating away.

5. Say to yourself, "Today I release my need for control. It no longer serves me." Breathe in protection and strength.

6. Say to yourself, "I will not carry my shame any longer. I will find healthy ways to handle my pain." Breathe out any shame and pain.

7. Continue to breathe in light and healing. Know that you are protected and that any feelings that may be coming up are safe to experience.

8. Slowly repeat the words, "I am not my addiction and I deserve recovery."

A DAY AT A TIME

As you have come to the close of this workbook, I hope I have led you on a journey to see the possibilities of living a life in recovery. Many young people don't take, or don't get to take, time out of their lives to be so introspective and to challenge themselves. Commend yourself for delving into your life and living it with intention.

You still face the challenges and decisions that come with moving into young adulthood, but you can now do it in a way that's clearheaded and values-driven. You will know you are living a life steeped in self-respect. Recovery is the greatest gift you can give yourself. Thank you for letting me be a part of your journey.

CLAUDIA BLACK, PHD, MSW, is a renowned addiction clinician, speaker, and trainer who is internationally recognized for her pioneering and contemporary work with addictive disorders. She has more than forty years' experience in the field of addictive disorders, with an emphasis on working with young adult populations. She is the recipient of multiple prestigious awards, and is author of more than fifteen books. She lives in the Seattle, WA, area.

More 🕐 Instant Help Books for Teens
An Imprint of New Harbinger Publications

DON'T LET YOUR EMOTIONS RUN YOUR LIFE FOR TEENS, SECOND EDITION

Dialectical Behavior Therapy Skills for Helping You Manage Mood Swings, Control Angry Outbursts, and Get Along with Others

978-1684037360 / US $21.95

JUST AS YOU ARE

A Teen's Guide to Self-Acceptance and Lasting Self-Esteem

978-1626255906 / US $17.95

THE TRAUMA AND ADVERSITY WORKBOOK FOR TEENS

Mindfulness-Based Skills to Overcome and Recover from Prolonged Toxic Stress

978-1684037971 / US $19.95

REVERSING THE SPIRAL OF DEPRESSION FOR TEENS

Simple Actions to Improve Your Mood, Boost Motivation, and Build the Life You Want

978-1648483479 / US $21.95

OVERCOMING SUICIDAL THOUGHTS FOR TEENS

CBT Activities to Reduce Pain, Increase Hope, and Build Meaningful Connections

978-1-684039975 / US $18.95

PUT YOUR WORRIES HERE

A Creative Journal for Teens with Anxiety

978-1684032143 / US $19.95

🌱 new**harbinger**publications
1-800-748-6273 / newharbinger.com

(VISA, MC, AMEX / prices subject to change without notice)
Follow Us 📷 📘 𝕏 ▶️ 📌 in ♪ ⓖ

Don't miss out on new books from New Harbinger.
Subscribe to our email list at **newharbinger.com/subscribe** 🖱